AF230564

PRAISE FOR
STRIVING FOR ANTIRACISM

"Speechless. Reading *Striving for Antiracism: My Imperfect Journey* is like being gently—but unmistakably—called to attention, heart first. Casey's words are deeply personal yet universally resonant, weaving vulnerability, courage, and unflinching self-examination into a narrative that is both profoundly human and urgently necessary. Through their story, I found myself reexamining my own assumptions, my own definitions of "goodness," and the unspoken racist systems I've lived within. Their ability to capture seismic cultural shifts through the lens of individual experience is nothing short of masterful. What I admire most is the honesty—with the reader, with the world, and with themselves. This is more than a memoir; it's a mirror. It's the kind of writing that lingers, that matters, and that will move people toward deeper reflection and change. I am proud beyond words to know the person behind this work, and even prouder to call them a friend."

—Tiffany M. Young
Founder and CEO of The Young Impact Group

"Casey has always known that story is a great transformer, especially when coupled with vulnerability. *Striving for Antiracism* is an honest, heartfelt, vulnerable look at the way White-bodied Americans experience the learning and unlearning of our White Supremacy Culture indoctrinations. For White-bodied coconspirators, we know the process is painful, embarrassing, confusing, and ultimately harmful to our friends who identify as the global majority (particularly when done without support). Casey's story, and their ability to tell it from a place of humility with an analysis and through the lens of racial equity, is a gift to our world, especially in today's climate. Casey is humanizing the experience of unlearning the bad bargains we never knew we were taught while extending a handout with resources, inspiration, and a compassionate hug. *Striving for Antiracism* is an invitation to other White folx to see ourselves in this cultural revolution, to join this journey toward a more inclusive society, to find our humility around racism, and ultimately to start learning how to talk to ourselves and each other about our often harmful participation in today's cultural zeitgeist and all its associated issues."

—Dayana "Dayo" Vice
Antiracism Strategist and Community Organizer

"In *Striving for Antiracism*, Casey embodies a rare and beautiful mix of confidence and humility that invites readers to imagine what becomes possible if we surrender our attachment to unjust power. With irreverent honesty and joyful humor, they reveal how discomfort can be fuel—not a barrier—for transformation. They meet us right where we are: steady, clear, and unafraid to name what's hard. Through achingly relatable stories, Casey makes you feel seen, while encouraging us to dismantle the fortress we White women have built to avoid reckoning with our role in upholding White supremacy. I'm in awe of the skill and care with which Casey calls us into our dignity and full humanity."

—Kristen Wright
Collaborative Governance Practitioner and Educator

STRIVING

FOR

ANTIRACISM

STRIVING

FOR

ANTIRACISM

*my **imperfect** journey*

CASEY TONNELLY

Publish Your Purpose
141 Weston Street, #155
Hartford, CT, 06141

The opinions expressed by the Author are not necessarily those held by Publish Your Purpose.

Ordering Information: Quantity sales and special discounts are available on quantity purchases by corporations, associations, and others. For details, contact the author at info@beyondthinkingwithcasey.com.

Edited by: Nancy Graham-Tillman, Lily Capstick
Cover design by: Jamie Ty
Typeset by: Medlar Publishing Solutions Pvt Ltd., India

ISBN: 978-1-955985-98-7 (paperback)
ISBN: 979-8-88797-235-0 (ebook)

First edition, March 2026.

The information contained within this book is strictly for informational purposes. The material may include information, products, or services by third parties. As such, the Author and Publisher do not assume responsibility or liability for any third-party material or opinions. The publisher is not responsible for websites (or their content) that are not owned by the publisher. Readers are advised to do their own due diligence when it comes to making decisions.

Publish Your Purpose is a hybrid publisher of nonfiction books. Our mission is to elevate the voices often excluded from traditional publishing. We intentionally seek out authors and storytellers with diverse backgrounds, life experiences, and unique perspectives to publish books that will make an impact in the world. Do you have a book idea you would like us to consider publishing? Please visit PublishYourPurpose.com for more information.

To our collective humanity:
May we remember that our liberation is bound together,
that our differences are not barriers, but bridges,
and that our capacity to care for one another is greater
than the forces that seek to divide us.
May this work be a step toward a world
where everyone can not just survive but thrive—
in dignity, in equity, and in love.

CONTENTS

Foreword xv

Preface xxi

Introduction xxv

CHAPTER 1: 9/11 AND MY AWAKENING OF PERMISSIBLE RACISM 1
Grief, Rage, and the Beginning of Racial Consciousness

CHAPTER 2: CALLED IN, CALLED OUT, CALLED FORWARD 7
Discovering I Could No Longer Pretend I Was Not Part of the Problem

CHAPTER 3: DANCING WITH DENIAL 29
From Righteous Anger to Rattled Awareness

CHAPTER 4: INHERITANCE 39
How Obedience, Silence, and Belonging Socialized Me Into Racism

CHAPTER 5: IN GOD'S SHADOW 63
Faith, Fear, and the Unholy Lessons of Racialized Religion

CHAPTER 6: THE CURRICULUM OF COMPLIANCE 89
How School Shaped My Understanding of History, Power, and People

CHAPTER 7: POP CULTURE, POLITICS, AND PROGRAMMING 115
Media, Memory, and the Making of My Mind

CHAPTER 8: WHAT THE F*CK DID I ABSORB?! 133
Reconciling Love, Harm, and Misguidance

CHAPTER 9: MY FRAGILITY EXPOSED 147
How My Fear of Being Seen as Racist Kept Me from Doing the Work

CHAPTER 10: I THOUGHT I WAS FURTHER ALONG 163
Confronting the Distance Between My Intentions and My Impact

CHAPTER 11: FROM WANTING TO BE GOOD TO CHOOSING TO DO GOOD 179
How Self-Reflection Rewired My Commitment to Antiracism

CHAPTER 12: A FRIENDSHIP I LOST, AND THE LESSON I WILL NEVER FORGET 193
Practicing Antiracism Is Not a Destination but an Evolution

CHAPTER 13: WORKING TOWARD EMBODIED ANTIRACISM 207
Letting My Body Lead Me to Braver Conversations, Harder Truths, and Real Growth

CHAPTER 14: NO ONE HAS ALL THE ANSWERS 215
Practicing Antiracism with Humility, Reflection, and Relational Accountability

Afterword 235

Acknowledgments 237

Appendix A: Glossary of Terms 241

Appendix B: 1980–1999 Extended Timeline of Some Major US and Global Events. 265

Appendix C: A Few BIPOC Women I Wish I'd Learned About (Sooner). 281

Appendix D: The Five D's of Bystander Intervention 293

Bibliography 295

About the Author 301

FOREWORD

*The most dangerous place for Black people
to live is in White people's imagination.*
—D. L. Hughley

Black Joy is sacred. Both ancestral and imminent. Black Joy binds us together across geography and time. It creates, connects, and makes us whole. It is equally ritual and radical, generating uncompromising resilience beyond comprehension.

My favorite Black Joy ritual is laughter—that uninhibited, full-bodied, deep belly laughter that erupts from unrestricted Black bodies, that laughter that makes you want to laugh. It's raw, rich, and vibrant. Wherever oppression lives, Black Joy makes space that is nourishing, replenishing, and soothing. It's a special kind of freedom to claim Black Joy, the personal agency to treasure what is deep and rich and soft in us.

Black Joy exists outside of White awareness. It's so far beyond the scrutiny of the White imagination that they call it magic, because anything the White imagination cannot grasp becomes fictional.

So, when D. L. Hughley told the world that the White imagination is a dangerous, violent, and deadly encounter, I couldn't stop laughing at his description. It wasn't just the irony of the joke; it was the look on the White faces in the audience trying to laugh off their discomfort. The White audience members were clearly confused because the White imagination assumes that its way of knowing, being, and seeing is the right way—the only way. It sees Whiteness as normal and universal, and everything else as a cultural footnote.

When I speak about the White imagination, I'm not just talking about fantasy. I'm talking about a force that is deeply embedded and constantly active, one that filters how White people perceive the world and, more pointedly, how they perceive us. It's the internalized myth that centers Whiteness as normal, neutral, safe, and good and casts everyone else as deviation, as risk, as "other."

The White imagination is not passive. It constructs, defines, interprets, and labels. It trains White people to see themselves as the default and the basis of all things. It constructs entire narratives about those of us who are not White, long before we have entered the room and introduced ourselves. The White imagination is delusion wrapped in convenient stereotypes and irrational fears.

The White imagination convinced a White woman in Central Park that she could summon the police as a weapon against Christian Cooper, a Black man who simply asked her to leash her dog. The White imagination drove three White men in Georgia to believe they had the right to hunt down Ahmaud Arbery. The White imagination justifies the bullets that killed Tamir Rice, Atatiana Jefferson, Eric Garner, and so many others. These were not accidents. They were the extremely deadly consequences of a White imagination that renders Black and Brown lives suspicious, expendable, and disposable.

The White imagination is dangerous when it believes that marching in pussycat hats is antiracist solidarity. The White imagination is dangerous when it believes that hiring Black leadership in your organization is antiracist change work. The White imagination is dangerous when it assumes that a book club is building antiracist awareness.

The White imagination is most dangerous when it believes that racism is something external—it's those people over there, those people who aren't as smart and progressive as you, the ones celebrating racist statues, the ones who summon racialized tropes, those neo-Nazis marching in khaki pants carrying tiki torches. It's those bad people, those hateful people, those who want to relive the days when the White imagination didn't need to control Black and Brown bodies because legislation and society did it on the White imagination's behalf.

In the following pages, Casey offers a piercing, unflinching examination of the White imagination and its distortion of White identity development. It is not an easy read, nor should it be. Casey invites us into the tension, grief, and rawness of what it means to live as a White person choosing to grow in a society that benefits from White complacency. Their reflections are merciless where they must be, tender where they can be, and always rooted in the belief that transformation is possible, but not without personal cost. They show us how White identity is not fixed but continuously constructed and that interrogating it is not only necessary but urgent.

I first met Casey over two decades ago when we were assigned as cross-racial partners tasked with providing antiracism training to nearly fourteen thousand city government employees. What we didn't know was how much we would learn and grow together over our twenty-plus-year relationship. Around them, I could breathe easier. I felt seen, and not for a version of myself that I needed to present but for who I am. I found Casey to be rooted in intention, integrity, and the values they've carefully shaped for themselves. Casey didn't seek applause, didn't pretend to be perfect, and didn't need external validation to feel whole. They owned their experiences and story fully, flaws and all.

Throughout this book, Casey shares and reflects on their story with the kind of gentle honesty that can come only from deep self-reflection and radical self-acceptance. Without defensiveness, without performative guilt, and without seeking absolution, Casey walks us through the deeply personal and profound political journey of examining what it means to unravel Whiteness from the inside out.

Through stories of family, culture, and history, Casey does what White readers are rarely asked, let alone required, to do: look in the mirror without turning away. Page after page, Casey dismantles their personal experiences with the myths of the White imagination, those dangerous figments that uphold White supremacy, justify violence, and obscure the very real harm Whiteness continues to inflict. They expose how Whiteness constructs itself as trustworthy, neutral, even benevolent while simultaneously erasing, exploiting, and invalidating the lives of Black and Brown people.

This book serves as an impressive and much-needed contribution to Whiteness studies. Serving simultaneously as a mirror and a map, Casey brings forward the work required to reconcile the White imagination, offering their White identity development journey as a reminder that true antiracist work begins when White people stop asking, "How do I not be racist?" and start asking, "What will I risk to dismantle what Whiteness built in me?" And not to be applauded, not to be consoled, but to face the uncomfortable truth that the delusion of Whiteness has always come at a cost to ourselves and to others. It's a recognition that empathy is not enough, that "niceness" is not absolution, and that we do not live in a post-racial world, no matter how many well-intentioned White people might wish it so.

It is White **ethnocentrism** that feeds the White imagination. Because Whiteness has always been centered in everyday experience, calls for equity feel like White erasure and a personal attack. That's why even well-meaning White folks stumble when conversations about race get too real. This work is not linear. It's not tidy. It doesn't offer neat solutions or soft answers. But what it does offer is something rare: an honest grappling with power, complicity, and the inner architecture of Whiteness.

Kyana Wheeler
Abolitionist, Antiracist Organizer,
Antiracist Champion

PREFACE

For most of my life, I believed I was one of the "good" White people. I was raised to condemn overt racism and White supremacy in its most explicit forms—slurs, hate groups, and blatant discrimination. And yet I absorbed the unspoken lessons that came with my socialization: racial stereotypes passed off as common sense, coded language that masked bias in neutrality, and a cultural lens that allowed me to see racism as an individual problem rather than a deeply embedded system in which I was complicit. I knew racism was wrong, but I didn't yet understand the ways I'd been shaped by it.

My journey with antiracism has been one of humility, self-forgiveness, and grace. Nearly two decades ago, I made the choice to step beyond my assumptions and actively engage in the work of unlearning racism, not as a theoretical exercise but as a daily practice in community and in my work. The process has been neither linear nor comfortable. Through my involvement with the City of Seattle's

Race and Social Justice Initiative, and later through founding my own coaching practice, Beyond Thinking, I've come to understand that antiracism is not a destination but an ongoing commitment.

This book is not a declaration of arrival. It's an offering of my lived experience—missteps, reckonings, and transformations alike. It's an invitation to others who, like me, have had to unlearn what we once accepted as truth and embrace the lifelong work of doing better. Unlearning racism is not about guilt or self-flagellation. It's about stepping into responsibility with courage, honesty, and a willingness to change.

I did not set out on this journey expecting to write a book. Like many White people raised in the United States, I was socialized to see racism as an individual failing rather than a system embedded in every aspect of our society. I was taught that overt racism and White supremacy were wrong, yet I absorbed racial stereotypes and coded language that reinforced harmful narratives. Since I prided myself on being "one of the good ones," I didn't realize that this mindset kept me from understanding my complicity in a system designed to benefit people who look like me at the expense of others.

I've learned that antiracism is not about seeking validation or proving our *goodness* but about recognizing how we're implicated in injustice and actively working to dismantle it. It means listening more than speaking, amplifying voices that have been historically silenced, and recognizing that discomfort is not a reason to disengage. It's about shifting from a mindset of defensiveness to one of accountability and realizing that change happens in community, not in isolation.

This book is a reflection on my journey, including my missteps, my learning, and my ongoing commitment to dismantling racism in myself and in the world around me. It's not a guide to perfection but an invitation to those who, also like me, have been shaped by a culture that resists this reckoning. The process of unlearning and relearning is lifelong, requiring vigilance, humility, and an openness to discomfort. It's in the difficult conversations, the willingness to sit with our discomfort, and the determination to act differently that true transformation happens.

As I look back on the pivotal moments of my journey, I see a pattern of gradual awakening, a process of peeling back layers of assumption and privilege, confronting hard truths, and choosing to do better. Some of these moments were painful, requiring me to confront parts of myself I would've rather ignored. Others were profoundly affirming, reminding me that this work is not about individual perfection but about collective progress. I share my experiences not to center myself but to offer a window into moving from passive awareness to active engagement.

For those beginning this journey, I encourage patience with yourself. There is no final destination, no checklist to complete, no point at which you'll be "finished" with this work. There will be times when you feel overwhelmed, when you make mistakes, and when you want to retreat. Keep going. Let those moments be opportunities for growth rather than excuses for inaction.

To those already on the path, I offer my gratitude. I have learned so much from those doing this work for far longer than I have, and I remain committed to listening, learning, and showing up in meaningful ways. Antiracism is not a solitary endeavor; it's a communal effort that requires all of us to engage fully and consistently.

To those who have challenged me, held me accountable, and pushed me to deepen my understanding, I thank you. Growth isn't always easy, and it often comes from the discomfort of being called in or called out. I'm grateful for those who've had the patience and courage to help me see where I still have work to do. This book is a reflection of that learning, and I hope it serves as a contribution to the collective efforts toward justice and liberation.

May we continue the work together, with courage, humility, and an unwavering commitment to justice.

With hope and solidarity,
Casey Tonnelly

INTRODUCTION

I never wanted to be a **racist**. I was always afraid of being called a racist,[1] afraid of being seen as a racist, afraid of being associated with racism in any way. I was raised to be a "good" person, a "good" member of society, and to be seen that way by others. I was raised to believe (overt) racism was bad, so if I was a good person and not overtly racist, then I wasn't racist. Right?

WRONG.

One of my first humbling moments of discovering my own racism occurred in my first job out of college. I grew up during the beginning and height of the AIDS epidemic. I could feel the fear my parents, my family members, adults, newscasters, and politicians had about this new and deadly virus. I heard it in their voices as they spoke or whispered about it and in their silence as they didn't speak about it at all. I heard it in random safety messages uttered with feverish

---

1. See appendix A for a glossary of terms.

urgency, such as "Don't sit on the toilet!" and "Get out of the pool!" and "Wash your hands with peroxide!" We rarely had conversations about what was going on with the virus, who it was impacting the most, or what was being done to keep people safe. We were driven by fear.

I was curious to know more about this new virus we were so afraid of and why we ostracized family members because of it. Years later, I was able to take multiple classes about HIV and AIDS in college. Once I learned what the virus was, how it was transmitted, and how it could be treated, I wanted to share the information with anyone who'd listen. I became a campus HIV educator, in part because, prior to college, I knew almost nothing about HIV and AIDS. I operated from the same place of fear of the unknown as my family, and with the assumption that people had to have done something wrong to become HIV positive.

On campus, I gained a reputation for always having an abundance of condoms with me for anyone who might need one. The New York State Department of Health came to the campus twice a semester and offered free and anonymous HIV testing, and I went and got tested with anyone who wanted support. Over the years, I got to know the HIV prevention program manager, a White woman, well, and when it came time to graduate, she encouraged me to apply to become a testing counselor in her program. I felt proud to be on her team and of the work we were doing, and I felt honored that she believed in me to be able to do the job. The position included outreach into higher-risk populations, HIV education, and pre- and post-test counseling. A huge part of my upbringing, particularly in my family and church, was about being of service, caring for my fellow human beings, and being present to support my fellow "man" who might be suffering.

That said, I was ill-equipped for the job. A short time after my onboarding, a new program manager was hired, a Black woman. As she settled into her new position, she asked each of us counselors, who were mostly White, about our connections and relationships with the communities we were entering. We were aghast. Most of us White counselors didn't have any such connection. We rotated visits to three clinics, and our outreach included visiting local jails, state-funded rehab and detox facilities, and areas with high levels of sex work—all within predominantly Black and Brown neighborhoods. We deeply cared about HIV and AIDS prevention and were committed to supporting everyone through the testing and results process. We were angered by the insinuation that because we were White, we weren't able to effectively do our jobs or serve these communities.

The resistance and anger I felt in my body were all-consuming. I could feel the heat that reverberated through my body every time our new manager was present. My defensive behaviors included silence, coldness, and avoiding her whenever possible. A quiet battle ensued between our new manager and the White testing counselors, and our interactions with her were icy and withholding. Eventually we were all replaced. Some left on their own, some were fired, and some transitioned to a different team. I was let go at the end of my probationary period and was angry, heartbroken, and embarrassed. I was angry at the new manager for thinking I couldn't do the job because I was White, I was heartbroken because I loved the job and felt proud of it, and I was embarrassed because I didn't want to tell others I'd been let go.

With time, space, reflection, and the development of a more nuanced racial analysis, I now look at this time very differently. The new manager was right to fire me. I didn't have any inkling of what the people we were serving experienced in life. I'd centered myself in the entire experience, believing I was good because I was helping people through a major life experience. I believed I was good because I was doing work many people didn't want to do, and I believed I was good because I wasn't shying away from people often vilified in society. I was also engaging in the work transactionally and centering how I saw myself, not our clients' experiences of the testing process or of me. The manager hadn't thought that I couldn't do the job because I was White; she knew I couldn't do the job because I lacked an understanding of racism, power dynamics, and various clients' realities.

I was devastated because I didn't want to believe I had caused additional harm to people who were going through an already potentially traumatic event. I was ashamed. I feared being judged by my friends and family. I was also embarrassed because I didn't want to be seen as a bad worker, a failure, or a bad person. Now I can see that I wasn't ready for that job. I didn't have the lens, analysis, or soft skills to connect with people, to be present with them, or to center them and their experiences. I can own that now without feeling shame, self-judgment, or guilt.

That didn't happen overnight.

It took me years to learn to like myself, let alone begin to love myself. I was raised and socialized as a female—an identity I never felt comfortable in—and to perform in a way that centered others' ideas and perceptions of who I was and who I was supposed to become. This taught me to be inauthentic. It taught me that there was no space for me, as I was, in my own life. It was one of the secrets I carried throughout my primary developmental years. I believed I was asexual for the first eighteen years of my life, but I understood that a heterosexual life was required of me to be permissible in my family and church.

People I loved and admired were suffering because of their secrets and shame rooted in societal stigmas, fears, and ignorance. Witnessing their suffering reinforced my hiding and masking of who I was, from others and from myself.

Secrets became the harbinger of my shame, guilt, and fear; my biggest fear was being ostracized and excommunicated from my family and church. I was afraid of being seen as unlovable, unworthy of consideration or care; I was afraid I was a mistake and disposable.

It took years of risk-taking in **antiracism** work to break those beliefs in myself. Antiracism work played a major role in transforming my beliefs, mindset, and behaviors. In my family, being queer was a straight (pun intended) pathway to hell, an abomination. For years I pleaded with my family to love me, trying to assure them that I was the same person. But that wasn't actually true. I was different. I became more authentic, and my authentic self disrupted their perceptions of who they thought I was and who I was supposed to become. For a time, this left me without a compass for life.

It was through antiracism work that I learned my silence, secrecy, and masking caused others harm, in addition to myself. The people I met and the community I made through antiracism work taught me that my "goodness" was not based on my straightness, assigned **gender**, or racial identity. They encouraged and supported me in examining what "goodness" even meant, and they challenged me to think more critically without villainizing or shaming myself or others. They engaged in conversations with me that were nuanced, heavy, and didn't rely on a binary way of thinking, such as good versus bad or right versus wrong, and they pushed me to expand on what I thought I knew. It was often uncomfortable for each of us, but we kept showing up for one another even when we didn't agree or even like each other very much. We were in this work together.

As my antiracism work and journey expanded into cultivating community, a whole new way of existing opened up to me. Exploration and expression were encouraged in art, in gatherings, in friendships, and in relationships. People's full identities—including my own—were welcomed, included, and protected, and that was the norm. I became part of a queer writing group that was multiracial, gender diverse, and accessibility oriented. We started every gathering with check-ins where people could share their racial identities, their pronouns, and access needs. We had agreements that supported **accountability** and learning, so more people were willing to speak up and receive feedback. It was like nothing I'd ever experienced before, and once I did, there was no going back.

Engaging in antiracism work challenged internalized stigmas I'd absorbed through societal and cultural assimilation, such as binary thinking of right and wrong and the belief that asking for help is a sign of weakness. This allowed me to admit to myself and others that I'd been traumatized by my childhood, family, and societal messages and that going to therapy did not mean I was "crazy." Going to therapy allowed me to untangle the complex emotions I was experiencing and acknowledge the defensive tools I'd developed that no longer served me, supporting the development of new tools in order to move out of survival mode. For example, I could love my family and also have firm boundaries with them.

Working in antiracism allowed me to discover and love my authentic self. This included reclaiming many of the messages ingrained in me during my primary years of **socialization**:

- I am loyal and dedicated to my chosen family. I have their backs, and they have mine.
- I have faith without being aligned to any one religion.
- I love learning, being curious, and asking questions beyond accepting what I am told to believe.
- I am rooted in love without conditions, demands, or requirements.
- I accept imperfections in myself and others.
- I believe mistakes happen; it's what we do when we learn we've made a mistake that matters.
- Joy and love are powerful when they're not prescriptive or conditional.
- Forgiveness of ourselves and of others is healing, no matter the result.

I spent my entire life trying to prove I was "normal" and "good" in an effort to maintain what I believed was the feeling of belonging. I was constantly shapeshifting and morphing myself into a version of who others wanted me to be, depending on the environment and who was around. I was the ultimate lemming. I did everything I was told to do. I delighted my family by being dependable and of service, I delighted teachers with my compliance, I pleased my priests by being devout and submissive, and I impressed my bosses by going the extra mile with a smile on my face. I was exhausted and miserable. Inside my mind and my heart, I knew I was someone else, not just the created version of me that was being groomed for society's approval.

When I came out to my family, it didn't go well. My father and my aunt tried to have me committed. This was the reason I waited until I was almost three thousand miles away from home before telling them. In New York, their hysteria about my coming out began with calling each other, their respective priests, and me. Family members inquired about who I'd told and whether I was playing a prank and demanded I take it back before we all became destined for hell. When they informed me that they were coming to get me so they could get me the help I needed at a **Catholic** hospital in New York, I had a full-blown panic attack. I was sweating, my heart was racing, and my body wouldn't stop moving.

As I paced around feverishly at work, I heard my name called over the loudspeaker to come to the front desk. I was working at the American Red Cross in Seattle at the time. I assumed I was about to get fired, as my life felt like it was falling apart. Barbara, the nicest and friendliest person I'd ever met, was working the front desk and asked me whether I'd seen her pen. I snapped back into the moment with the banality of her question and had to ask her to repeat herself. She did. My mind and heart zipped between two realities: my family trying to have me committed and my colleague asking for help finding a pen.

After a few moments of us crawling on the floor looking for her pen, she said, "We hear you're having a rough day," looking at me with gentle brown eyes as she placed her hand on my shoulder. Barbara was a Latter-Day Saint. I assumed that my family had called the front desk and she was now helping them snatch me.

I pushed myself away from her and yelled, "Don't touch me!" My fight-or-flight response was strong, and my entire body tensed up as I retreated from Barbara with my hands firmly extended in front of me.

She backed away and gently said, "Okay, okay, no one is going to touch you."

I stood up, and she pointed to the front door, where I saw twenty or so colleagues standing with their jackets and bags. I felt surprised and disoriented as my eyes feverishly moved from left to right.

Harold, the director of emergency services and a career naval officer, shouted in his gruff voice, "C'mon, kid. We're taking you out."

Barbara leaned down just over my ear and said, "We've got your back. No one's gonna take you against your will."

I was in a state of shock and disbelief. I could feel the tears welling as my heart slowed and my body began to relax. It was the middle of the afternoon, the collection of people at the door never hung out together, and Barbara and Harold rarely spoke to each other. Bao, a Vietnamese immigrant and operations manager, invited me to hide at his place with his two kids, enticing me with their karaoke machine. Franklin, a Black man and our most popular first aid instructor, offered to crash on my couch, as he had his black belt in Judo. Marta, a Mexican immigrant who managed the language bank, told me how she was very close to God and knew for a fact that he loved me.

This cross-racial, multi-faith, and gender diverse group of people caught me when I felt my world crumbling, simply for sharing a bit more of my authentic self. At a time when I felt the beginning of my excommunication from my family and faith, these folks let me know I belonged and was not alone. In antiracism work, no one cared that I was queer. No one cared that I was **nonbinary**. No one judged me for my past, my upbringing, or my family. The only question asked of me was, "Are you committed to antiracism?"

I was. And I still am.

Transformation takes work. Transformation takes time. Transformation takes risk-taking and sometimes failing, and that takes courage and humility. Transformation allows space for us to become more authentic versions of ourselves. The beautiful part of transformation is that there's no going back.

In this book, I'll walk you through my imperfect journey in antiracism work. I'll share stories of discomfort in learning and awakening **awareness**, stories of my cringeworthy resistance to those moments, and stories where I felt embarrassed. I'll share stories of pushing past my own shame, guilt, and fear and stories of moving from learning to mindset and behavioral shifts. I'll also share stories of when I stayed silent and when I took risks and stories of when those risks paid off, when they didn't, and when they had no impact at all. In doing so, I'll share with you some of the mistakes I've made in unlearning racism, learning about antiracism, and engaging in antiracism work. I share these stories not for you to judge or scoff at me but rather to invite you to experience the reality that who you are, at this moment in time, is needed to help advance antiracism initiatives, conversations, and efforts. Not your perfect self, but *you*. As you read through the stories I share in this book, I hope you reflect on your own. Our stories don't need to be the same in order to be relatable.

So who am I, and what is my background in antiracism conversations and work? I am a White, middle-aged, nonbinary (socialized female), queer, neurodiverse, and privileged human. Admittedly, in my first two and a half decades of existence, I had an unnuanced and binary understanding of racism and how it functioned in people, interpersonally, institutionally, systemically, and culturally in the US. I was raised and taught to believe that racism is mostly a part of our history and only in the South. I was raised and taught to believe that if you worked hard, you could have the American Dream, which at the time meant a union or public service job that allowed for a steady and comfortable middle-class existence. I was raised and taught to believe that most people are good and care about their fellow human, and I conformed to the societal standards of goodness. And I was raised and taught to believe that everyone has a fair chance in our country.

Through my personal and professional antiracism work over the last twenty years, I've worked to make that last part a reality. My intentional antiracism work started accidentally. Admittedly, I didn't want to do this work. As you'll read later, I fell into it as a workaholic focused on achievement and advancement in an effort to prove my worth to myself and my family. Starting to develop new relationships was what changed me, and these relationships became the foundation of my antiracism work. I learned how to listen to others when they share their stories, their realities, and their experiences: listening for the emotions behind their words and the tension in their voices, listening for what matters to them most. I also learned to share openly, vulnerably, and authentically by being honest with myself and others about what I think I know, what I was taught, what I don't know, and where my learning edges exist.

In these relationships with my chosen family and friends, I've been able to engage in antiracism conversations through coaching, caucusing, workshopping, and strategic planning. One of the most powerful tools I've developed over this time is my curiosity. I've become an incredibly curious person, a person who asks questions and questions whether we're asking the best ones. I've become a person who values our collective humanity, a person who values kindness, care, and compassion without conditions. There are a few questions I frequently ask myself to support these new ways of existing:

1. Who has the **power**? (In all spaces, environments, and relationships?)
2. How are they using their power? (To benefit themselves, to maintain or gain power, to maintain or gain influence, or for the population at large?)
3. Are people harmed by how the power is being utilized? (Are their voices and experiences acknowledged? Included? Heard? Valued?)
4. What are the alternatives for eliminating and mitigating these harms?

Black and Brown leaders, especially Black and Brown women, have been calling on White folks, especially White women, to operate in solidarity for centuries. They've been asking us to continue to show up for **equity** and to engage when the White, frequently male, backlash to any equity efforts presents itself. This is my invitation to my fellow White folks, especially White women, to lean into the discomfort; push past fear, shame, and guilt; and stand in solidarity with our Black and Brown sisters, brothers, siblings, and those fearing for their safety and wellness.

I wanted to write this book from a place of vulnerability, authenticity, and my imperfect learning, relationships, and experiences. From what I've seen, most of the books written by my fellow White folks on topics related to or about antiracism, racism, **inclusion**, and equity have come from either an academic place or as a subject matter expert. Let me be clear: I have read many of these books and learned from them, but at the same time I want to see more narratives discussing the complexities, pain, and ugliness that can come from both discovering racism does exist within oneself and working to excavate it. That's the book I wanted to write, using myself as a case study.

This book shares my work in discovering, excavating, and processing my own racism. I share experiences and conversations that pushed me to examine what I thought I knew and where I needed to learn more. I give invitations to think and behave differently, in ways that reduce the harm Black and Brown people experience. I wanted to write a book that exposed my imperfect journey in discovering and engaging in antiracism work, and that includes how I make mistakes, how I strive for accountability, and how my commitment to supporting antiracism work, activists, and leaders is unwavering, while I am fallible. And I wanted to write a book that supported other White folks in their antiracism journeys and to let them know they aren't alone.

Over the last two decades, I've had the privilege of engaging in antiracism work within government, community, corporations, and nonprofits. Across industries and environments, a common exchange occurs:

White person: "Just tell me what to do."

Black, Brown, or multiracial person: "You have to do the work."

There is no roadmap for this work, no one way to do it, no gold star or arrival point. Leaning into antiracism requires us to commit to an evolving experience and to learn in a multitude of ways.

This book is not a one-stop shop for becoming **antiracist**, nor does it have all the answers—far from it. I am imperfect. My upbringing was imperfect. My healing, learning, and growth have been imperfect, as has my antiracism journey and work. Most importantly, my commitment to building an equitable society is steadfast and firm.

Will you join me in imperfectly leaning into antiracism?

Chapter 1

9/11 AND MY AWAKENING OF PERMISSIBLE RACISM

Grief, Rage, and the Beginning
of Racial Consciousness

On September 11, 2001, at the age of twenty-two, I was working alone at one of the New York State Department of Health's clinic sites as an anonymous HIV testing and prevention counselor. Little did I know how my life would change when news came over the radio at 8:46 a.m. that a plane had struck a tower at the World Trade Center. The radio hosts remarked, "What a moron, didn't they see the building? It's a beautiful, sunny day, and that building is huge." Unalarmed, I continued to set up the clinic for the day, pulling out paperwork, needles, vials, and bandages. Seventeen minutes later, the second tower was struck by another plane, and the people on the radio went silent. Silence on the radio can be very alarming, particularly when you're in a state of shock and desperate for information.

My 9:00 a.m. appointment didn't show up that day, so I went into a hallway with other clinic staff to congregate, share information, and comfort each other. On one small TV in the staff kitchen, we watched as the south tower collapsed. Gasps and other expressions of dismay rippled through the kitchen and clinic. Moments later, the anchors on the morning news program announced the crash of Flight 93 in Pennsylvania. It was immediately apparent that New York and the US were under attack—a shocking and terrifying experience, mainly because we, as Americans, aren't necessarily accustomed to experiencing war-like conditions on US soil.

Panic took over at work. The office doors sprang open, and people rushed out screaming about getting their kids or needing to head into Manhattan to help as medical personnel. My manager called my office to tell me that because the target was unclear and because we were in a government building, they wanted everyone to leave immediately and go home.

As I made my way home, horns blared, people screamed and cried out, emergency sirens went off in every direction, and American flags flew out from windows. It was chaos. I broke out into hives as I began to think about friends and family who worked in the towers or close to them. I went to my dad's apartment. He worked in building 7 at the time and wasn't home. I was there only a few moments when the phone rang. It was my older sister, who was a teacher at a local high school. She asked me to wait for our father because she was going to stay at the school until all her students were picked up.

My father came home the next day. My sister cried in relief of his return, while some of her students lost one or both of their parents. Everyone in New York knew someone, most of us multiple people, who died that day. We were a devastated city, state, and country.

New Yorkers are a proud people with a fighting spirit, a fact that remained steadfast in the days, months, and years following the attacks of 9/11. There was a lot of love, chipping in, and showing up for others who'd lost loved ones that day, a collective energy that was both powerful and healing. However, what failed to receive much news coverage during that time was the open and permissible hate and violence being perpetrated against anyone who was perceived to look like they might be Middle Eastern. New Yorkers were driving their cars onto sidewalks and hitting fellow New Yorkers who might be Middle Eastern, and Middle Eastern store owners were attacked and had their stores vandalized or destroyed, yet I noticed there was little media coverage or public condemnation of those attacks. It was heartbreaking. Many of the victims of these assaults had also lost loved ones who worked at the World Trade Center.

That day and the months following wrecked me for a multitude of reasons and in a variety of ways. It was the first sizable domestic terror attack I'd experienced within proximity of my person. Everyone around me, including myself, was on edge, assuming another hit was just around the corner. I was grieving people I'd gone to high school and college with, and so were my friends. We attended weekly memorials, fundraisers, and community resiliency events together. Widespread pain, wailing tears, omnipresent anger, and frequent and sudden outbursts filled the streets. I was traumatized by the outright violence and racism I saw and heard from my fellow New Yorkers, including **Islamophobia**.

A few months later, my boyfriend at the time, Xavier, decided he wanted to go to paramedic school. I was selfishly concerned about the amount of time he'd be unavailable and jealous of the idea that he'd be experiencing something new and exciting. These reactions ultimately changed the trajectory of my life forever because, in search of a new adventure of my own, I decided to join AmeriCorps National Civilian Community Corps, the most intensive and paramilitary AmeriCorps program, for eleven months of volunteer service.

I was based in Charleston, South Carolina, and worked on various manual labor service projects throughout the Southeast. I knew very little about the South, but as a New Yorker I felt superior to it. I was excited to listen to "people talk funny." As you can imagine, I was quickly humbled. With my very thick Long Island accent in the South, *I* was the one who talked funny. I also learned a lot about how racism can function, and not because racism doesn't exist in New York (it does) but because it functioned differently than in New York: It was more explicit, visible, and palpable.

At the end of my first year of AmeriCorps, Xavier and I lovingly decided to break up, and I moved to Seattle, Washington, to start my second year of AmeriCorps with the American Red Cross. I was further humbled as I continued in this new role, responding to local home fires and working intensively with the Red Cross language bank. Many of the victims of the fires, including residents who spoke English, wouldn't talk to me unless a volunteer from the language bank was present. When people are devastated or traumatized, especially within **minoritized** communities, it's unsurprising that they find greater comfort in speaking to someone who looks like them and understands their **culture**. It also made me feel awkward, inept, and useless. A small example of how multiple things can be true at the same time.

After college, in my early and mid-twenties, I was on track to be the good person I was expected to be in this life. This trajectory was drafted long before I was born. My family invested time and resources to ensure I reached these expectations, my church laid out the pathway for a righteous life, and my school provided the foundational information to achieve the status quo. National and global events provided opportunities to reinforce the narratives I learned, and my exposure to multiculturalism was limited. However, the life I was designed for and expected to live was not rooted in truth, reality, or authenticity.

I was committed to being a good person, and in my mind a good person wasn't a racist. The reality was that I *was* a racist; I just didn't know it yet.

Chapter 2

CALLED IN, CALLED OUT, CALLED FORWARD

*Discovering I Could No Longer Pretend
I Was Not Part of the Problem*

In 2007, while working as an inclusive outreach specialist at the Seattle Office of Emergency Management, I was sitting alone at my desk in the back of the office. My desk phone rang, and the caller ID showed it was the Seattle Police Department (SPD) headquarters. Our office was technically part of the police, but aside from our email signatures, we rarely had any connection with them. The running joke was that we were the ignored children of the department and liked it that way.

The first thought that ran through my mind as I stared at the SPD name scrolling across my phone was, *What the fuck?* I ignored the call and waited for the voicemail light to go on to see whether they'd leave a message. They did. The message requested a callback. I didn't make one. They called two more times that day, but I ignored them both. I blew it off, assuming it was a donation call for either the chaplaincy or their nonprofit, the Seattle Police Foundation, as those were usually the only calls I received from them.

The next day they called again, and I thought to myself, *Ugh, let's just get this over with and be done with it,* so I picked up the phone. An older gentleman with a husky voice introduced himself as Captain Perkins and, in a barely audible whisper, informed me that he'd been attempting to reach me for days. The only response I could muster was, "Okay." He then stated, "You're a trainer for us, and you work with different people, correct?" The phrasing of his words befuddled me, and I was unsure how to respond. I didn't need to come up with anything to say because he continued speaking: "Great, you're going to help train our officers and all staff on anti-profiling. We'll be sending out a survey this week to identify the 'Train the Trainer' dates." Then he hung up.

I panicked. I'm confident I stopped breathing for at least ten seconds with my mouth frozen open. The stillness of my body didn't reflect the frenzy of energy and thoughts racing through me. I didn't want to do this. I was terrified of being in a room with armed officers who didn't want to be there while having challenging conversations.

Once I was able to move again, I sprinted to my director's office. Ellis was smart, calm, strategic, and widely respected. She happened to be one of the only female emergency managers in the country and was also queer. I admired her. As I stood in her doorway with all the color drained from my face, my eyes as wide as they could go, and my mouth still open, she spun her chair around, looked at me with a kind smile, and said, "They called you, huh?" My mind was spinning at the idea that she knew they'd be calling me and hadn't tried to get me out of this situation. "This will be good for us in budget season," she offered.

Screams of *FUCK!* ran through my head and likely out of my mouth. I felt grossly aware of how ill-equipped I was to be leading antiracism conversations. I didn't think I had the proper knowledge, the right skills, or the right credentials. I was afraid I'd get it wrong. I was also scared that my not-good-enoughness would be exposed to my colleagues and my boss. I assumed I'd feel embarrassed and deeply ashamed of myself and then probably get fired, and that idea felt unbearable, insurmountable. After scrambling to get out of facilitating the trainings and pleading with my boss to no avail, it was announced that the Train the Trainer program would not begin for ten weeks. The additional time felt like a lifeline because it gave me the chance to try to get out of the commitment and to skill up. In those ten weeks, I took every city and community course I could find on antiracism, inclusion, and courageous conversations.

With Train the Trainer only four weeks away, I met with someone from the Seattle Office for Civil Rights Race and

Social Justice Initiative Team who called me in and out, and it changed my life. Cherese, an older Black woman who exudes warmth and perceptiveness, asked, "Have you ever complained about policing?" This was at a time when stories had come out about officers pulling women over and pressuring them to engage in sexual activity to avoid a ticket or arrest. This was happening in various parts of the country, so yes, I had some complaints about that. She said to me, "People have been banging on this door for hundreds of years, and you just got an open invitation to walk through. Are you really not going to take it?"

She was right. I still didn't want to, but I realized that I needed to walk my talk of not being a racist. It was like getting punched in the stomach. I wanted to be good. I wanted to be enough. I wanted to be liked and to feel as though I belonged somewhere.

Time moved very slowly in the days after that conversation because I was deep in reflection on her words, which had me reexamining who I thought I was. Being vulnerable with other people was not a strength of mine at the time. I thought not knowing and not having answers was a sign of weakness, so I was processing things alone in my head, a strategy I relied on in my childhood to feel safe.

I soon learned that I'd be cofacilitating with an officer from the SPD training unit. A few days before the first training, I'd lost my appetite. I couldn't put anything into my body without it violently coming back out from one end or the other. I couldn't sleep, each minute feeling more like a year with all the panicked thoughts running through my mind: *This is going to be bad. I might be attacked. What if someone pulls a gun?* I lost five pounds within two weeks before the first training. I was twenty-eight, stood five feet tall, and weighed barely ninety-five pounds, so I didn't have weight to lose. My body was responding as it did when I was a child, and food was weaponized: good children get something to eat; bad children do not. My body adapted to periods of hunger and a lack of nourishment, enabling me to get through difficult times.

For a week before the first training, I read my notes from the Train the Trainer program and curriculum aloud while looking in the mirror, occasionally pausing to give myself a pep talk to boost my confidence. A few nights before that first training, I asked my roommate and trusted neighbors to heckle me as I practiced my welcome, closing, and transition points. I laid out what I was going to wear for the first session as a reminder that when I feel confident in my clothes, I feel more confident in my skills. I selected my red pants, a turquoise button-up shirt, and a yellow tie, a combination that helped me feel grounded, joyous, and most like myself.

As I walked toward the training center door the next day, nervous energy flooded my whole body. My mind raced with thoughts about not being ready; about not being able to handle any aggressive or passive-aggressive behavior, answer questions, or support my cofacilitator; about the training going so badly that I'd get fired. I kept telling myself to maintain a game face, to not give any impression of nerves or discomfort, but my insides were screaming.

I swiped my employee badge to unlock the front door. It didn't work. I tried again, to no avail. I couldn't get into the building. After a few moments, three older White male officers in plain clothes approached. "Having trouble getting in?" one of them asked, his face grimacing. All three officers had their sunglasses on even though it was a cloudy day. They didn't wait for my response before swiping their employee badges in front of the sensor to unlock the door. "After you," said the officer who first inquired whether I was struggling to get in. "We don't have a lot of visitors come down here."

My year living in the Southeast helped me learn the coded language of Southern hospitality and politeness. For example, "Where y'all from?" means "You're not from here," "How long y'all staying?" means "When are you leaving?" and "Bless your heart" is as versatile as the word "fuck," depending on the context. This initial interaction with these officers made me hyperaware that I was an outsider and did not belong there.

As I walked into the training room, I was relieved to see my cofacilitator, John. I'd been strategically paired with him because he was an officer from the training unit, and sworn officers often won't listen to anyone who isn't a sworn officer. This practice of importance hierarchy is shared in many professions, from education (administrators, teachers, and support staff) to healthcare (administrators, doctors, nurses, and support staff). However, hierarchy takes on new levels in law enforcement. John was of mixed race and highly educated, and he'd served as an officer for fifteen years. He was always kind to me and helped me feel less alone, yet his demeanor changed constantly when other officers were present. He smiled less, interrupted people more frequently, resisted ideas or concepts that differed from the status quo positions of line officers, and wouldn't talk to us civilians unless absolutely necessary. I felt terrible for him. To feel like he had to act or be a certain way around his peers seemed so out of line with his authentic self, and acting to feel like he belonged seemed exhausting.

A deputy chief soon walked into the room, and all the officers' demeanors changed to quiet, stoic, and disciplined. Chief Harvey Thompson was in his mid-fifties, tall, and fit, and he had excellent posture and always a warm smile. Officers continued to acknowledge his arrival by saying, "Chief." He walked up to me, said hello, and extended his hand to shake mine. "You must be Casey," he said. "Good to meet you. Thank you for helping us put these training sessions on." I was a bit taken aback, but this was my first real insight into the disconnect between leadership in headquarters and the line officers. He nodded his head, indicating I should follow him to a side hallway of the training room. "How you feeling, Case?" he asked.

In most circumstances when someone I don't know shortens my name to a nickname to indicate closeness or intimacy, I cringe. My nerves were pretty high, and the tension in the training room was thick, so I didn't mind as much. "I'm curious to see how this goes, Chief," I said, not knowing how to actually respond.

He nodded his head and gently smiled at me before sharing, "Don't let them beat you up too much. Most of them think of this as a punishment. They think we don't support them, but they fail to realize this is an investment in them to do their jobs better."

Nodding back at him and wanting to appear confident, I said, "Thank you for the encouragement, Chief. Honestly, I don't plan on letting anyone beat me up at all." Meanwhile, in my mind I repeated, *Don't shit your pants. Do not shit your pants. Under no circumstances do you shit your pants.*

The chief chuckled and nodded his head again, then said, "Good for you, Case, I'll check in on you later."

As the training began, so did the more active resistance. Multiple officers refused to fill out their name tents, a few put their heads down to sleep, two kept their headphones in, and one sitting in the front with his feet on the table had a newspaper up, open, and fully expanded. We were met with various responses when requesting engagement:

"You don't need to know my name."

"Everyone here who matters knows who I am."

"This is mandatory training, and I'm here; that's bad enough."

"You're wasting our time; we could be at the gun range. That would be a better use of our time."

It felt like being in a romper room.

We began the training with a table game, and there was lively engagement. However, as John and I walked around the room, we realized that no one was actually playing the game we'd provided. We cut the time short to ask what officers were discussing at the tables.

Silence.

Then, the officer reading the newspaper aggressively slammed his paper down on the table and declared, "I have something I wanna say."

This is when my New York Italian family ancestors rose up inside me: "I bet you do. Is it about the article on page two or sixteen?" My posture changed, the tone in my voice shifted, and my accent even emerged. His mouth opened wide under his bristly mustache. "No?" I interrupted, "Then I don't want to hear it. You've been reading the paper since we started and are not engaging here. If you want to share, put your paper down and participate." He crumpled his paper and placed it in his backpack. Inviting him to share, I asked, "What is it?"

"These training sessions are a waste of time. You don't know what it's like to do our job, what it's like out there, and these touchy, feely, be-nice trainings are just PR bullshit. There, I'm done."

I took a pause and a breath before responding, "You're right, I don't know what it's like to be a cop. I never wanted to be a cop, for many reasons." Turning toward the group, I continued, "You can't deny there's a disconnect between police and multiple communities, that some communities don't trust you, that some communities won't talk to you, that when communities don't trust or talk to you, your job is harder, right? So, why wouldn't you want to reduce that disconnect?"

There was a lot of pushback indicating that the fault lay within the communities. Some officers stood up, yelled, pushed chairs around, cursed, and called John and me various names. "Does the community get paid to engage with you?" I asked, receiving grumbles as responses. "It's your job to build trust and relationships in communities. It's not their job to give you the benefit of the doubt when they haven't received it. You're getting paid to be here. Every profession has standards and accountability measures. We're not trying to have a 'touchy-feel-good' conversation. We want to have a real one, but y'all ain't showing up for it. This behavior from y'all is exactly what the community thinks of you. To me, you're proving them right."

With that we took a break, and when we came back the romper room antics stopped. Participation was limited, but we managed to complete the first training. At the end of the day, Chief Thompson came to check on John and me. "How'd it go?" he asked.

John responded, "Better than expected, Sir. We all made it out alive."

"Good, that's good," said the chief. "How 'bout you, Case, you ready for the next one in two days?"

"No, but I'll be here." Cherese's question about being in or out anchored me in that moment.

Chief Thompson and John smiled and gave me literal pats on the back. I was depleted in a way I had never experienced before. I asked the chief to make sure my badge would work by the next training and left in what felt like a haggard state. I took my bike to the bus stop and went straight home, was in bed by 5:30 p.m., and didn't wake up until my alarm went off at 6:00 a.m. the next day, still wearing my clothes from the day before.

Cherese had texted me to wish me luck the morning of the first training and again to check in while I was on the bus home. "How'd it go?" she asked.

"What's the bar of measurement we're using?" I said, feeling like I didn't know how to describe that first day.

"That bad? How are you feeling?" I could feel the warmth in her texts.

"I don't know. It was hard, really hard. There were a few moments that felt potentially powerful, but I feel like I'm about to get my PhD in facilitation." I didn't know how to answer her questions.

"That's probably true. Let's find time to debrief this week. Get some rest." Her offer to connect and debrief helped me feel less alone and reminded me that I was becoming a part of something much bigger than these training sessions.

I continued to attend antiracism courses held in the community by the People's Institute Northwest, the Coalition of Anti-Racist Whites, Showing Up for Racial Justice, and Minority Executive Directors of King County (MEDKC) to address feeling ill-prepared, ill-equipped, and much more ignorant than I'd originally thought. My colleague Carol, a middle-aged, fifth-generation Asian woman who was two decades older than me, heard that I was attending a training session organized by MEDKC and asked to join me. I was thrilled to attend with someone I knew, and she and I often had robust and in-depth conversations. We were in the same role at the Seattle Office of Emergency Management and shared an office.

Carol often referred to herself as a "banana." I didn't know what that meant, so when I asked she stated, "I'm yellow on the outside and White inside." I still didn't understand. The description felt offensive and heartbreaking to me, but I thought to myself, *This is her identity and claimed expression; who am I to question or challenge her?* I asked her whether it would be okay if I asked some questions. Very bubbly, friendly, and kindly, she casually responded, "Oh, yeah, I'm happy to share; I'm an open book."

After a few moments, I asked whether she ever felt she had to hide parts of herself. She sat back in her chair, looked up at the ceiling as she thought about it, exhaled, and responded, "Huh." She then shared that she had experienced name-calling as a kid and that she struggled with dating for a while, as many men saw her only as arm candy or a potential wife. Snapping back into her bubbly self, she also said she didn't think about it much more as an adult. She elaborated that she and her husband had been together for almost twenty years, and they mostly just enjoyed spending time together.

This conversation felt very uncomfortable in my body. Speaking directly and intimately with a colleague and friend about racism and our different experiences with it was new territory for me. My heart felt heavy, like when something disappointing happens. My mind still felt curious and confused by her use of the banana expression, but I wanted to respect her boundaries about it, so we moved on to talking about work.

I still reflect on this conversation, which helped me explore our different lived experiences, and I think about the respective geographies we grew up in. As a Midwesterner, Carol was socialized to prioritize civility over discomfort, and as a New Yorker, I was more comfortable with direct questions. I also reflect on our age difference and how that impacted the racial terminology our generations heard and used, as well as on the different pressures we experienced to assimilate, the experiences she shared that reduced her humanity to tropes, and how that impacted the way we self-identified.

For the MEDKC training, we decided to drive together, as our boss had approved our attendance on a weekday and we could use one of the department's cars. The training occurred in a historic building located in the heart of the city, which housed multiple nonprofits, community groups, and various events. We found a parking spot just a few blocks away, which felt like a good omen to us because such an occurrence was unheard of in Seattle. We were both smiling and chatting as we approached the training location, happy to be out of the office without having to take time off to attend. The sun was shining in January, and Mount Rainier was visible, indicators of a good day in Seattle.

Our training room was located on the first floor, just next to the main entrance of the building, making it very easy to find. There were round tables set up throughout the room, with five or six chairs tucked under each one. Carol and I, both trainers and facilitators, knew quite well that participants usually liked to sit in the back or near an exit door. Since we were the first to arrive, we chose to sit at the center table in the middle of the room. One of the facilitators looked up and said, "Hey, alright, alright, good to see you. Thanks for not sitting in the back corner. Y'all wanna come up front?" Carol and I awkwardly laughed before Carol responded, "It's okay, we like it here." The facilitator smiled on one side of his face, lightly nodding his head. That small interaction exposed both our eagerness and our discomfort.

There were two facilitators for the day. The gentleman with whom we had our pretraining awkward interaction was a Black leader in an area nonprofit, and he was paired with a younger woman who was also a Black leader but in a different area nonprofit. The gentleman was somewhere between fifty-five and sixty-five based on some of the personal stories he shared, and he had a strong presence. He was sharply dressed in a dark-gray three-piece suit, a vibrant bow tie, and a pocket watch. The younger woman was only a little older than I was, and she was tall and slender. She wore a dress with geometric shapes that cinched around her stomach, a gold belt, and gold earrings that matched and hung just over her shoulders. It felt like we were in the presence of great-ness, like someone you admire and never thought you'd have the chance to meet. They were both volunteers with MEDKC.

Slowly, the room filled with mostly White participants. There were a few other Asian women, a couple of Latino men, and one Black woman. Carol and I were the only government workers present; everyone else worked for non-profit organizations. After introductions and an icebreaker, the facilitators explained the first thing we were going to do was define **race** and racism so we could engage in conver-sation with a shared definition. My first thought was, *Who doesn't know these definitions?* Admittedly, I was feeling a little smug at the time.

As they began, they also normalized that everyone had some **bias**. The gentleman facilitator elaborated, "We have narratives about children, young adults, middle-aged individuals, and older individuals, right? We have narratives about churchgoers and non-churchgoers, right? And other religions? We have narratives about tall people, short people, thin people, muscular people, curvier people, right? Those don't even include how each of those people are portrayed on TV or in the movies, if they are at all, right? Nor does it include any experience we may have or have not had with any of these people."

Heads nodded with every word he said. He had us. The facilitators celebrated with each other that the room agreed with the statement that everyone had bias. They then defined race as a social and political construct.[2] At the time, I'd never heard it described that way and didn't quite understand. Carol wrote in her notebook and slid it my way: "Have you heard that?" I looked at her and shook my head. We weren't the only ones. The female facilitator called on one of the affirming, head-nodding participants to break down the definition they'd shared. This affirmed my decision not to nod at the definition to prevent being called on.

The inquiry led to a truly powerful conversation about history, exploring how, why, and when laws are written and enacted, and the discussions included asking us who benefited from these laws and who was suppressed by them. The facilitators shared how laws rarely state explicitly who the intended beneficiaries are or who consequently becomes disenfranchised. None of this had ever been discussed in my schooling.

Once we all understood and agreed to the definition they shared about race, we were ready to move on to define racism. Both facilitators stood in front of the room and jointly facilitated this part. The gentleman got us started: "We agree that we all have bias, yes?"

---

2. Ta-Nehisi Coates, "What We Mean When We Say 'Race Is a Social Construct,'" *The Atlantic*, May 15, 2013, https://www.theatlantic.com/national/archive/2013/05/what-we-mean-when-we-say-race-is-a-social-construct/275872/.

"Yes," we replied.

The gentleman raised his chalk to the air, signaling agreement, and the young woman took the lead, asking, "We agree that race is a social–political construct, yes?"

We had discussed this at length, so with vigor we collectively responded, "Yes."

"Excellent, excellent," she said as she turned to write on the board. The gentleman facilitator added that, like any social or political construct, race benefits some, harms others, and leaves others experiencing both benefits and harms, yet those harmed are rarely named explicitly. We instantly got quiet, and the facilitators allowed us to sit uncomfortably in silence for what felt like an eternity. I could feel my body wanting to fidget, but I didn't want to bring attention to myself.

The female facilitator broke the tension with a playful tone in her voice. "Are y'all losing your minds right now because you never thought of it that way, or did we not explain that right?"

More silence, including from me.

The gentleman began writing on the board:

BIAS + SOCIETAL POWER = RACISM

An older woman spoke up, "So are you saying all White people are racist?"

The facilitators smiled and didn't respond immediately, allowing us to absorb this definition. I was immediately livid. I could feel the defensiveness rising inside me, and all I could think was, *This is bullshit!* I cognitively shut down and barely remembered the rest of the training. All I could think about was myself. The thoughts zigzagging in my brain were about my own experiences: *I had an abusive parent. I'm queer. I've been unhoused. My life is hard, and I've worked my ass off to get out of those situations. How could I be racist?*

Once we left the training room and approached our car, I unloaded my resistance onto Carol. She comforted me. Being much more composed and graceful than I was, she shook her head and just said, "That was too harsh. I didn't like that. I didn't think that was fair." We were both quiet the rest of the time as I finished my cigarette in the parking area.

We drove back to the office, discussing how we could avoid talking about training with anyone until we had time to process the day. We wanted the weekend to think about what we would say to our boss and any colleagues who might ask about the training on the following Monday. Our office was located far away from everyone else, so we devised a plan to drive to the back of the building so no one would see us return. We were supposed to return the car keys to the front desk, but that area was where all our colleagues sat. So, we would quickly and quietly pack up any items from our office that we needed for the weekend, leave the department car keys on Carol's desk, then sneak out the back. Carol would call the front desk on her drive home to report that she'd forgotten the keys on her desk, a believable lie since she always forgot to return the keys to the front desk.

After we successfully implemented our plan, I walked home as I usually did. I was particularly grateful that the walk was primarily uphill because it allowed me to work out the rage that was swirling through my body. I felt tense. My jaw was so tight I was practically grinding my teeth, and my shoulders were holding so much tension that I occasionally felt the backpack straps brushing against my earlobes. My hands were gripped in fists as I pumped my arms walking up the hill. The definition they shared that day meant that I was a racist. That felt vehemently untrue to me. I had used the "N" word casually with a friend once in high school and felt wrong saying it, so I never repeated it again. I was engaged in antiracism work at my job, had begun to push back against my racist family members, and hated racists! That day, I walked up those hills so fast that it was the only time it didn't take me a full hour to get home.

Once home, I began to debate with myself between the lessons I'd learned that day from the facilitators and what I wanted to be true. I paced heavily back and forth across my bedroom, arguments ricocheting through my mind: *That is THEIR definition of racism, not mine. I know racists; I am not one of them. I have friends who are Black. Today was bullshit. I am not racist.*

I told myself these messages because I thought they were what I needed to hear. But even as I repeated those words in my mind, something gnawed at me. I wasn't sure whether it was the facilitators' definition of racism I was trying to reject or the unsettling feeling that, deep down, I knew they might be right. My pacing grew more frantic, my breath shallower. I wanted so badly to believe that my actions, my intentions, my discomfort with overt racism meant I couldn't possibly be part of the problem. And yet why was I so resistant?

I clenched my fists again, this time not from the cold or the weight of my backpack but from something deeper, something I couldn't yet name. I needed to prove them wrong. I needed to prove myself right. But no matter how hard I tried to push the thoughts away, the rage inside me only grew.

I wasn't just denying their definition of racism, I was fighting against something in myself. And I didn't know what it was or how to stop it.

Chapter 3

DANCING WITH DENIAL

From Righteous Anger to Rattled Awareness

I decided to take a shower after I confirmed to myself that I was not racist and before going out dancing with some friends. I imagined the water from the showerhead rinsing off the trainer's definition of racism, and I watched as it swirled down the drain. Once I got out of the shower, I turned on some music and danced around my apartment to help adjust my mood. I tried to convince myself that I felt okay, but there was a volcano of furor erupting inside of me. I lived alone and was stewing in my resistance at the idea that I could be racist.

Actively trying to ignore those feelings, I began to pick out my outfit and found my favorite T-shirt, orange with blue stripes on the shoulders and sleeves and a cartoon duck on the front. I borrowed it from a friend years earlier and never returned it, and it helped me feel connected to them. I decided to wear it under my fancy dress shirt because I wanted and needed to feel more comfortable in my own skin. With a final glance in the mirror and a slight hair adjustment, I was ready to be with my friends, dance, and feel vindicated.

The bar was underground, very dimly lit, and an anything-goes kind of place, as long as things were consensual and not impeding on others' use of the space. It felt liberating to be there. I could see my friends standing in the corner, which was unofficially designated as the area for queer-identified folks. I said hello to everyone gathered there, placing my jacket and backpack by them before heading to the bar to order a drink, which I craved after that training. I felt a sense of relief being around others who were like me and in a space where the focus was on music, dancing, and fun. I made eye contact with the bartender as I stood at the back of the line. He was the regular Friday bartender, and we'd developed a sweet rapport with each other. As he held up a bottle of whiskey and pointed at it, I nodded my head yes and smiled at him. He winked at me and poured a double, which would be waiting for me as the line shrank down. I could feel my nervous system relaxing. I was at one of my favorite places to dance with my friends, a place where I was well-known. My facial muscles began to unclench, I began to smile, my breath slowed and flowed with greater ease, and my shoulders settled down.

I spotted a young woman I was immediately drawn to. I hadn't dated much since Xavier and I broke up, and I had come out to my family only two years earlier. As I navigated my family's disapproval, I focused on my work, having decided that I had no time for dating. I chose to avoid the woman. I felt uncomfortable enough that day and was not about to add a rejection to it. Instead, I approached a friend of a friend standing in the corner, Mae, a coworker of one of my core group of friends. She asked me the question I'd been waiting for since the training ended: "How was your day?"

I knew this was an opportunity to share my experience from the day and receive the agreement I was seeking. "It was a little rough."

Mae immediately offered me physical comfort by placing her hand on my shoulder. "What happened, Casey?" she asked.

I walked her through the lead-up of the story with why Carol and I were going to the training before sharing the definition of racism as "bias plus societal power."

Mae's jaw dropped before she exclaimed, "That's fucked up!"

I felt vindicated.

Mae pulled over her sweetie, Kaplan, and shared the story I'd just told her. Kaplan scrunched their face up while shaking their head no before offering, "That is such crap, dude. I hate that shit. I'm so sorry you had to experience that."

As the affirmation of my experience and reaction continued, I felt more and more validated. Once I shared my story and received the assurances I desired, I felt emboldened to share with others. I began working my way through the group of people standing in our corner of the room, mostly to continue receiving the acknowledgments I was seeking. A few people turned away when I shared, while others stayed quiet and stared at the floor. However, those who were engaged were on my side, and that was what I wanted and needed to feel assured of my goodness.

Before I knew it, I was back-to-back with the intriguing woman from the bar. I felt fascinated by her but was also nervous about introducing myself. I hadn't had these feelings for anyone since I started to have feelings for Xavier almost a decade earlier. This person was the cutest human I'd seen in a long time. She wore a short blue dress with flower patterns that twirled as she moved across the room and on the dance floor. I overheard her laughing before we met. I admired people with big laughs, as I often only said, "That's funny," while barely cracking a smile. As our backs continued to bump into each other, I realized I'd have to introduce myself at some point. It would be weird to be with the same group of friends and avoid doing so, like I'd initially hoped. Before I turned around, she was out on the dance floor with another friend, and I could see that it brought her so much happiness; she was beaming. I was enthralled.

"That's Ariana," my friend said to me.

"What?" I responded.

"I see the way you're looking at her. I haven't seen that before; it's nice. I'll introduce you when she comes back from dancing," he offered.

Panicked and trying to play it cool, I shrugged it off. "That's okay," I said. My friend chuckled and shook his head at me.

As Ariana skipped her way back to our corner, my friend introduced us and said that I wanted to dance with her. Ariana looked into my eyes intensely, in a way that felt too personal for my comfort. I was numb and in disbelief that my friend said I wanted to dance with her, but she offered me a crooked smile as she extended her hand to me. My heart raced, and I could feel myself start to sweat. I rubbed my hands on my pants to ensure I didn't grab her hand with a sweaty palm. As our hands connected, my mind began to rattle with disastrous thoughts and warnings: *Don't squeeze her hand too hard. Don't forget the steps. Don't hyperventilate. Don't seem too excited. Don't seem uninterested.* I was able to calm myself down by remembering I had a good story to share as a conversation starter.

Time felt frozen as we stepped onto the dance floor. As we began to dance together, she asked how my day went. I thought to myself, *This is it; I can share my story about the training, and we can be appalled together.* Based on the reactions others had when they heard my story, I was ready to have a rich conversation with Ariana. I assumed that like the other White people I'd talked to, she would be comforting. As I shared the definitions I learned at the training with as much charm in my voice as I could muster, I noticed her head nodding in agreement. I hadn't finished explaining the definitions when she jumped in matter-of-factly with, "I agree with that definition. That tracks with everything I've seen. Don't you agree?" Inside my head all I could think was, *Oh shit. This is not what I expected to happen.*

I tried explaining myself: "Yes, and I had a hard life and had to work really hard to get out of it."

With calmness in her voice, she said, "I'm sure you did. Did anyone say you didn't have to work hard?"

My mind swirled. My body panicked. Nobody had said I didn't have a hard life or that I didn't have to work hard, so where did that point of contention come from? Why couldn't all those things be true? It was true that I had a hard life; I had to hustle and work my ass off to have stability and safety. I agreed that racism was a social–political construct, that we all had biases, that a part of the construct included laws that benefited some individuals over others, that institutions cater to some over others. And I agreed that systems have been designed to allow White people to "pull themselves up by their bootstraps" and change their circumstances but did not offer the same opportunities to Black and Brown folks.

After our dance ended, we hugged, and she said she wanted to dance with me again. That made me happy, but my mind had begun to fall into the abyss of conundrums. How could I agree with those statements but reject the statement that racism was bias plus societal **privilege**? How could I feel vehemently opposed to and offended by racism when Black facilitators shared their truths? How was it so easy for me to ignore and dismiss their definition yet be so open to exploring it when Ariana said it? My body and mind were completely overloaded. I needed to leave the bar and go home.

I gave my whiskey to a friend and said a quick farewell to the group. I was dumbfounded by how that conversation with Ariana had affected me. I went dancing to receive comfort from my peers, but what felt more genuine and impactful was the accountability Ariana provided. There was too much to process from the day.

Once I was back home, I collapsed onto my bed and stared at the ceiling. The quiet in the room was a necessary balance to the chaos in my brain. I needed to examine my anger. I'd been feeling so angry at the audacity of the facilitators to imply I was racist while I agreed with everything else they'd said. I was angry that my goodness was being called into question, although that was never said. I was angry because racists were bad, bad people went to hell, and I was a good person aiming to get into heaven. I was angry at the idea that everything I'd learned and believed might not be accurate, at having to consider that racism was not just something external to me and that I was infected with racism without knowing it. I was angry because it wasn't good enough that I didn't want to be racist, and I was angry to have faith and pride in a society that would allow and perpetuate racism. And I was angry because the facilitators were right, because I hadn't seen the racism they described, because I didn't *want* to see it, because I'd been ignoring the racism they described and I had witnessed in my life. I was discovering how little I knew or understood about racism, especially my own, and I was discomfited.

Mostly, I was angry at myself because I realized my perception of my goodness was nowhere near good enough and that, in fact, I was a racist. I had no understanding that racism existed in multiple forms and operated at various levels, each one shaping me long before I ever had the language to name it. I didn't know that racism could be internalized without my consent, normalized without my awareness, or expressed through behaviors I'd been taught to see as neutral. I didn't realize that racism could be quiet, polite, or masked as "common sense." I only knew the caricatured version of racism—the "bad people"—so I never had to consider that it lived in me, too.

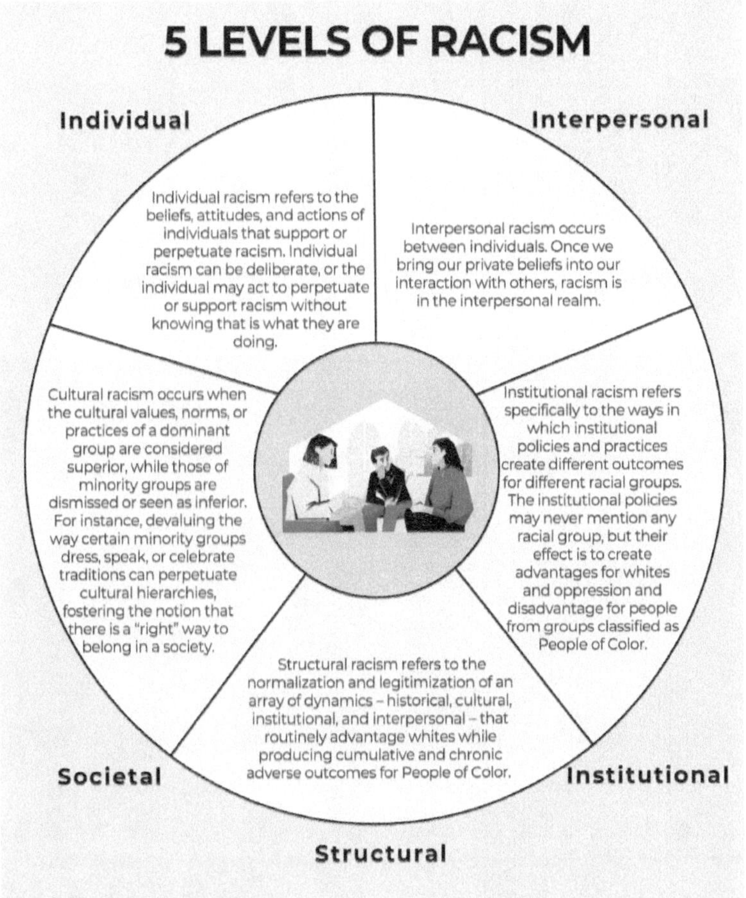
5 LEVELS OF RACISM
Individual
Individual racism refers to the beliefs, attitudes, and actions of individuals that support or perpetuate racism. Individual racism can be deliberate, or the individual may act to perpetuate or support racism without knowing that is what they are doing.
Interpersonal
Interpersonal racism occurs between individuals. Once we bring our private beliefs into our interaction with others, racism is in the interpersonal realm.
Cultural racism occurs when the cultural values, norms, or practices of a dominant group are considered superior, while those of minority groups are dismissed or seen as inferior. For instance, devaluing the way certain minority groups dress, speak, or celebrate traditions can perpetuate cultural hierarchies, fostering the notion that there is a "right" way to belong in a society.
Institutional racism refers specifically to the ways in which institutional policies and practices create different outcomes for different racial groups. The institutional policies may never mention any racial group, but their effect is to create advantages for whites and oppression and disadvantage for people from groups classified as People of Color.
Structural racism refers to the normalization and legitimization of an array of dynamics – historical, cultural, institutional, and interpersonal – that routinely advantage whites while producing cumulative and chronic adverse outcomes for People of Color.
Societal
Institutional
Structural

Figure 1

Chapter 4

INHERITANCE

*How Obedience, Silence, and Belonging
Socialized Me Into Racism*

I was not born a racist, but I was raised to be racist through socialization. Racism was poured into me from the moment I took my first breath. The embedding of racism in me did not take place through one person, one event, or one experience, nor was it always done overtly or consciously. It was a holistic approach, and it occurred like this:

- Through the language that was used in my childhood home.
- Because of the stereotypes my immediate and extended family stated as if they were facts, such as who was a "crook," who was "dirty," or who was "not very smart."
- By witnessing the behavioral changes my family exhibited depending on who was present. Did we cross the street?

Did we say hello? Did the adult I was with pull me in close, or did they need to keep tabs on me?

- By hearing White people refer to individual People of Color as "a good one."
- Through the news, such as how people were described, who was worthy of compassion and the benefit of the doubt, and who was presumed to be a criminal or guilty.
- Through TV shows, movies, and books. Who played the good guy on TV? What did the bad guys look like? Who were the victims of the bad guy? Adding a layer of sexism, if a female character was included, did she have a meaningful role? Was her sole role for sexual objectification, as a victim, as someone in service to the main characters, or as a prize for the good guy at the end?
- Through singing nursery rhymes and songs selected for school concerts.
- Through the reinforced history lessons I received throughout my schooling.
- When I observed who was in positions of leadership and authority in school, in businesses, and in our church.
- By being told who could and could not be trusted.
- By learning who was "like me" or my family and who was "not like me" or my family, the indication being that anyone "not like us" was a danger.

- By living in a predominantly White town and having limited and primarily transactional relationships with non-White people for almost all of my childhood.
- By not talking about race or racism outside of its historical context.

Culture, as defined by the Center for Advanced Research on Language Acquisition for the Intercultural Studies Project, is "the shared patterns of behaviors and interactions, cognitive constructs, and affective understanding that are learned through a process of socialization."[3] Some of the influencing elements of culture can include geographic location, language, education, food, music, art, economic philosophies, gender norms, gender roles, religion, storytelling, political structuring and philosophies, architecture, and more. In cultural anthropology, cultures are often categorized in three ways: guilt culture, shame culture, and a culture of fear.

Socialization is "the process of consciously and unconsciously learning norms, beliefs, and practices from individuals, media, and institutions about who does/does not have

---

3. "What is Culture?" Center for Advanced Research on Language Acquisition (CARLA), accessed May 28, 2024, https://archive.carla.umn.edu/culture/definitions.html.

> power and privilege as it relates to social identities and how the self is positioned in relationship to these identities; how we are supposed to act."[4]

I was born in 1978 on Long Island, New York, to two complicated, imperfect human beings who carried a lot of trauma, had limited resources, and were trying to survive life. They were born to four complicated, imperfect human beings who were born to eight complicated, imperfect human beings, all of whom carried their own individual traumas, some collective, and none of whom would admit to or talk about any of it. The manifestation of their traumas presented in a myriad of self-harming ways, including alcoholism, domestic violence, depression, avoidance, and hate. Intergenerational trauma shaped me even while it was never talked about explicitly.

The first pillar of my racist socialization is my family of origin in New York. I was raised to be a "good" person, someone who'd be accepted and permissible in mainstream society, someone who'd abide by the written and unwritten rules of US society, someone who'd make my family

---

4. Definitions, quotes, and examples are compiled from many sources, including Andrea Ayvazian; Andrea Smith; Black Girl Dangerous; Class Action; Kathryn Mathers; Dr. Wade Nobles; Peggy McIntosh; *Love, Race and Liberation*; Barbara Love; OpenSource Leadership; Racial Equity Tools; Robin DiAngelo; Colors of Resistance, *Challenging White Supremacy*; Isaac Giron; Anne Braden; Wikipedia; Barbara Major; and the People's Institute for Survival and Beyond.

feel proud. Because my goodness reflected their goodness, I was a reflection of them as parents, family members, society members, and Catholics. My trajectory for becoming a good person was predetermined before I was even born. I wouldn't cause any problems, I wouldn't complain, and I wouldn't seek attention. Instead, I listened to adults and did what I was told, end of story. I was also quiet and respectful to those who were deemed good or held a respected position of authority in society.

I absorbed many messages about being good without "good" being clearly defined for me. The dos and don'ts of demonstrating my goodness varied based on the environment I was in, the adults present, and whether there were additional respected figures there to witness and validate my goodness. I learned to look family members in the eyes and to initially make eye contact when encountering a priest, then look down to demonstrate reverence and humility. I learned to look at my teacher's face but not their eyes to demonstrate paying attention without being disrespectful. I learned to say hello to people accepted by society, such as our fellow church-goers, but to turn away from those who were unhoused and deemed dangerous. Generally, I learned that racists were bad and that we were good people, so we weren't racist. Beyond following rules like this, I lacked clarity on what being good meant or how to achieve it. One lesson I learned was that the only way to determine whether I was good was if others defined me as such. Another lesson I learned was that my obedience predominantly established my goodness. I may not have been clear on what it meant, but I knew I desperately wanted to be good, or at least be seen as good.

In New York, we were raised to believe that New York was the center of the world and better than everywhere else. Being a New Yorker is an identity all on its own, and locals are expected to have great pride in that identity. At the time, you were a good New Yorker if you lived in one of the five boroughs; understood key parts of New York history, such as when the Brooklyn Dodgers left New York (1957) and when the Empire State Building was built (1930); were always prepared with a quick comeback; and had the needed street smarts to navigate any situation. My family prided themselves on being *true* New Yorkers.

My grandparents and great-grandparents emigrated from the "old country," specifically Ireland and Italy, in the early 1900s. They longed for the food, music, and people of their home countries while railing against those governments for corruption and cruelty. In their countries of origin, they'd starved from famine and poverty, authoritarian whims imprisoned them, and their life expectancy was abysmal. They came to the US in the hope of a better life, or at least a survivable one. Their stories of **oppression**, resilience, struggle, and excruciating and dangerous working conditions have been passed down through generations in my family to instill the characteristics of hard work, gratitude, perseverance, and pride into each of us descendants. This is how our family absorbed the message and believed in the bootstrap mentality of the American Dream. Their story is not unique. This is common for immigrants who come to the US from around the world.

My Irish relatives escaped British rule by sneaking onto a boat across the Atlantic, and my Italian relatives had to renounce their Italian citizenship in order to leave. Some had to leave behind their parents, siblings, spouses, and children; some had to sleep on the sidewalks while they looked for work and affordable housing options; and some lost more weight from their already emaciated bodies because food sources weren't as available as they'd believed. All had bittersweet memories of arriving in New York.

The Irish side of my family was once considered the largest family on Long Island. My Irish great-grandmother, Deirdre, married my great-grandfather George when she was sixteen, and they had twenty children. For many generations in our Irish Catholic family, birth control was unacceptable, called a sin by our priests and faith leaders, and we were told it was against God's will. Deirdre was pregnant for the last nineteen years of her life. She died in childbirth at the age of thirty-six.

After her death, her children were left to raise themselves, which led to many complex and unhealthy dynamics, including various forms of harm, addiction, and criminal engagement. My grandmother Beatrice was raised by her older siblings and often experienced abuse and neglect. I believe this contributed to her becoming one of the most mean-spirited and cruel people I've ever encountered. She would berate my mother and her siblings constantly, whether privately, publicly, or in front of everyone in the family, and she created instruments, such as an old brush with some of the bristles replaced with nails, to hit people or "brush" their hair with. She'd also demand that her family serve her and cater to her every need. For example, she insisted that my sister and I be dropped off at her home to clean her house top to bottom, rub her feet, and do any chores or errands she needed completed. I hated being around her, especially when she ate. She always talked with food in her mouth. Many of her meals included a sauce, dressing, or gravy, and I have vivid memories of her putting more food inside her mouth than it could handle while she chewed and spoke unintelligibly as the liquids sloshed out the corners.

Her husband, my grandfather Hermit, was often drunk and would pass out or pretend to be passed out to not have to engage with his family. It wasn't uncommon while in his presence to hear him whisper, "Psst. Hey kid, go grab Grandpa another beer out of the fridge." That was the most interaction I ever had with him.

Being around my Irish grandparents and family helped me cultivate a great deal of empathy and compassion for my mother, knowing who raised her. My mother, Mara, was an incredibly talented artist and painter who was charismatic, charming, and compassionate to those outside of our home. Though she, too, was desperate to be seen as good and good enough by others, inside our home was chaotic and dangerous. She lashed out at my sister and me about any perceived injustice she'd experienced, how one or both of us had embarrassed her by an action or inaction, or about something entirely made up. Throughout my childhood, my mother was diagnosed with many mental health issues, including schizophrenia, bipolar disorder, narcissistic personality disorder, paranoid personality disorder, and antisocial personality disorder. Whenever she received a diagnosis, she lashed out at the doctor or psychologist before setting her sights on us.

This was in the 1980s and 1990s, when mental health and wellness weren't common or encouraged topics of conversation. Stigma related to mental health was ingrained into our society. Where I lived, you were either "sane" or "crazy"—that was it. If you fell into that second problematic category, you were ostracized, avoided, and feared. Our church also didn't believe in mental health or illness. The messaging they shared was that "crazy" was the descriptor for people who rejected God, "lost their way," or "listened to the devil." This societal practice prevented my mother from continuing care once a diagnosis was provided. She needed help—in some ways she wanted help—but the fear of being exposed as imperfect kept her suffering in silence.

As a child, I was immensely confused by loving my mother deeply, being petrified of her, and waiting on edge for her next act of cruelty yet fiercely desiring to protect her from having her mental illness exposed. The guilt and shame I felt by not being able to help her or being good enough for her crushed my soul and spirit. Whenever we were outside of our home, I glued myself to her side, in part because I never wanted her to feel alone and in part because I didn't want her to abandon me, which she threatened often. I will never know how painful and terrifying it must have been for her to live her life that way.

For us to be seen as a normal and good family by our church community, our neighbors, the teachers and parents at our school, and within our own family, we learned to conceal our truths. We learned that to be accepted by our communities and the pillars of socialization, we had to hide our realities and wear acceptable societal masks.

The dysfunction on the Irish side of my family was rampant. One year for the family Easter gathering, I was incredibly sick with a high fever and wanted to stay in bed. My absence would reflect poorly on my mother as a mother, according to her family, so my mother insisted I attend the day-long activities. When we arrived at her sister Siobhan's house, I immediately went to lie down on the couch and pulled the blanket over me. At some point, my younger cousins approached me, wanting to play as we often did during family gatherings. This time I told them no because I felt too sick and didn't have the energy to play with them. Shortly after that exchange, my cousins returned with my aunt and my mother, who were both flushed with anger. As they approached, Aunt Siobhan yelled, "You hit my kids?!"

This jarring accusation was disorienting. My brain felt fuzzy due to the fever, but I knew that hadn't occurred, as I was barely moving on my own. "No," I mustered as I remained on the couch. "I just said I couldn't play with them."

Undeterred in defending her kids, she proceeded to pull me off the couch and began kicking and punching me. My mother stood by watching as she continued to drink her soda.

Blood started to flow out of my mouth and nose, and as I pleaded for her to stop, my cousins confessed. "She didn't hit us, she didn't hit us, we lied!" they screamed while tears ran down their faces. My aunt stopped, and she and my mother turned and walked back to the rest of the family members without saying a word.

After this event, my grandmother, my mother's siblings, and their spouses and children pretended I didn't exist. No one spoke to me. There was never a place for me at any table, and they hung up the phone if I answered. But I was still required to attend family functions. It was awkward, demoralizing, and uncomfortable, but it also allowed me to witness the manifestation of how different family members held trauma and coped in their own unhealthy ways. I could watch who slowly and steadily became intoxicated throughout family gatherings; observe who frequently came late, left early, or called at the last minute to say they weren't attending; notice who avoided whom or always took the opposite stance of particular people; and track who competed with whom to demonstrate superiority over the other and who avoided the inevitable disagreements, arguments, judgments, or fights. I could also witness the venom in their words as they narrowed their eyes and tightened their mouths while spewing stereotypes and slurs as commonly as the words "the" and "and." I was glad to be invisible to them because I was scared by their ability to dehumanize people and wish them harm.

The Italian side of my family was also quite large. My Italian great-grandmother, Antonella, stopped speaking Italian when she arrived in the US to fit in and be accepted by her neighbors. The only exception she made was that when her children would argue, she'd burst out loudly singing Italian operas to break up the fight. My grandmother Grace and her four siblings all lived within four miles of each other, and between them they had fifteen children. Any gathering, holiday, birthday, or Sunday dinner on this side of my family had at least fifty people in attendance.

My father, William, is the eldest of three siblings, with twelve years between him and the youngest. My father's life and role in his family changed dramatically with the devastating death of his father, Gabriele, a firefighter who died of a heart attack in 1971 in Harlem while responding to a call. This loss influenced my father's parenting style. He both provided for our home financially and avoided being present in it whenever possible. I always thought of his parenting style as "detached attachment," meaning being present without being there. My earliest and happiest memory of my father is when I was around four years old. I'd spent the day with my mother at home, tending to her needs and absorbing her wrath, and was ready for reprieve. I heard the loud engine of my father's 1970s-style brown Plymouth Duster approaching our home, and I ran out the door and across our front lawn wearing pink shorts, no top, and plastic rosary beads around my neck. He chuckled, leaned down, and scooped me up. In my earliest years, I felt safer when he was around. As our home became more chaotic, he spent less and less time with us there, which made me feel less safe at home and around him.

My grandmother Grace went to church services almost every day. The most wonderful person I experienced in my childhood, she was loving, kind, generous, and caring. She hosted Sunday dinners most of my early life and had an open-door policy: her door would literally remain unlocked-while she cooked all day, the scents of her pasta, sauces, and meats wafting through her block. It was common for more than sixty people to walk through her home on a Sunday. Some relatives and neighbors would stay all day, while others would drop by to grab a plate or wait for a meal.

Grandmother Grace always wore her light-gray apron those days, including when she finally sat down some ten to fourteen hours later. She'd check in on everyone who walked through the door to see how they were doing and ask whether she could alleviate any hardships they might be experiencing, either by giving them food to take home, giving out clothing if needed, or handing them some cash. She even lent her car to members of her community who needed to get to dialysis appointments. I once witnessed her unplug her microwave and give it to one of my aunt's friends who was struggling financially because she was leaving an abusive partner, and my grandmother promised to drop off food every week to support her. She embodied everything positive I learned in church: having generosity of spirit, helping anyone in need, and building community.

She also paid dues to and believed in the mob—and operated by and respected their rules. I remember learning at an early age that family was the most important thing in life, and you protect the family at all costs. If anyone was perceived to be a threat to our family, murder was a supported option. A common phrase used by our family to demonstrate acceptance and inclusion was, "I'd bury a body for you." If I or one of my cousins brought a date to a family function, at least one person would come over to shake their hand, look them in the eye, and say something like, "Nice ta meet ya. If you hurt this one, I got a gun and a shovel, and your body would never be found." It was confusing to experience love and care through threats of violence.

One tenet of our family was to be wary of anyone outside of our bloodline unless they'd been vetted by a trusted family member or shown themselves to be someone who could be trusted. It was crucial never to say or reveal anything about anyone in the family to outsiders. I was told early and often never to trust or talk to the cops. Another tenet was to never lie to anyone in the family. A number of these lessons directly conflicted with other messages within my pillars of socialization. Murder is a sin in the Ten Commandments of the Catholic Church, cops were the good guys or heroes in normative American culture, and the Catholic Church, my family, my schooling, and mainstream society condemned lying and secrets. Yet my family required these behaviors in order to be seen as good and acceptable.

My uncle Enzo, who's my grandfather Gabriele's brother, and his wife, Lucia, doted on my grandmother Grace after my grandfather's passing. Enzo and Lucia were a great couple, the only couple in my family I saw who were happy and genuinely enjoyed each other's company. They were fixtures at Grandmother Grace's house. They chain-smoked, drank cocktail after cocktail, played pranks on each other, and organized poker games where the pot consisted of favors such as cleaning cars and running errands for others. They were affectionate and generous but horribly racist. At several family holidays, Uncle Enzo sat down next to me and pulled his eyelids up, down, and straight back, telling me that was how you could identify different **ethnicities** within the Asian community. Then he'd have me mirror his eyelid movements to ensure I did them correctly.

Most of the relatives in my grandparents' generation were openly and persistently racist. Listening to how they spoke about non-White racial identities or any other "outside" demographic was intense. The stories they told always included slurs, stereotypes, and racist jokes. They spoke words I was told not to say, told jokes I was told weren't funny, and shared stories based on stereotypes intended to evoke laughter. These moments were often followed by tense silence until someone changed the subject. I felt uncomfortable, but I was taught to listen to and respect my elders. This pattern of behavior instilled in me the lesson of "Do what I say, not what I do." Even as I was instructed to say nothing, I absorbed the messages and language of my elders.

One year, as my parents, sister, and I were driving away from a holiday gathering, I asked about this pattern. My dad was driving, my mom was in the passenger seat, and my sister and I were in the back of the car. My parents loved the oldies station, so music from the 1950s and '60s was always playing on their car radio. During commercials my mother lowered the volume, so when the radio went quiet, I asked my parents why our elders spoke that way and why no one stopped them. My parents explained that they were "from a different generation" and "things were different back then." When I asked again why nobody stopped them, both my parents warned me not to be disrespectful and advised me to "just leave it be" because the older generations wouldn't change their ways. These warnings prevented me from interrupting racism within our family for more than two decades and encouraged me to stay silent when overt racism was present.

My parents' racism was more hidden. They used slurs but not in public, and they told racist jokes but only in trusted company. They didn't blame all their woes on Black and Brown people, but they also didn't want Black or Brown people to move into their neighborhood. They didn't avoid television or music by Black people, but they did share and believe stereotypes about Black and Brown people. They didn't have Black or Brown friends, they winced in horror if any of my older cousins dated a Black or Brown person, and they casually encouraged my sister and me not to date Black or Brown people. It was there. I was listening to and absorbing racism both directly and indirectly through coded language and speech—a truth I could not ignore.

My racism developed in me before I was able to form my conscious values or determine how I defined what "good" and "bad" meant. It was hard to imagine that the foundation of my racism was rooted in people I loved, people who provided a sense of belonging. Memories I cherished and relationships I valued were seeded in racism as well. For a time, I allowed myself to believe that I couldn't possibly be racist. I didn't think, talk, or act like my grandparents' generation, nor like my parents' generation. I used their racism as the measurement for my own, so if I wasn't like them, then I wasn't racist.

Both of my grandfathers eventually secured union jobs and remained with them for the rest of their lives. At the time, this meant they could afford a living wage to support their families in single-income households. Throughout much of the labor movement of their time, White laborers often excluded Black and Brown laborers from negotiations, agreements, and contracts, thereby securing safer working conditions, reasonable working hours, and fair wages for themselves. This resulted in Black and Brown laborers being paid less and having little to no union benefits.[5] And this wasn't the first time people in power pitted cash-poor White people against Black and Brown people to quell the power

----

5. James Gilbert Cassedy, "African Americans and the American Labor Movement," *Prologue Magazine* 29, no. 2 (Summer 1997), https://www.archives.gov/publications/prologue/1997/summer/american-labor-movement.html.

of the people when they worked across differences. During Bacon's Rebellion from 1676 to 1677, indentured servants[6] and enslaved people fought together for the government to recognize their humanity and address their overall welfare. Those in power understood the threat of a united, oppressed people, so they fortified a racial hierarchy in the Virginia Slave Codes of 1705, which legally and socially created a class system: White, Christian, land-owning men at the top, White European indentured servants in the middle, and Black and Brown people at the bottom.[7] Unfortunately, this **social oppression** was not taught to me in school.

My grandfathers also both served in World War II. After the war, they were able to access the GI Bill benefits, including job assistance and loan support, to purchase a home. After World War II, at least one million Black and Brown soldiers struggled to access the GI Bill benefits they were entitled to due to redlining, a federal government initiative that began in the 1930s to address the housing shortage while also perpetuating racial segregation. The initiative created suburban housing where White folks could work with realtors and banks to secure loans. Black and Brown

---

6. Per *Merriam Webster's New Collegiate Dictionary*, 11th edition, an indentured servant is a "person who signs and is bound by indentures to work for another for a specified time especially in return for payment of travel expenses and maintenance."

7. Edmund S. Morgan, *American Slavery, American Freedom: The Ordeal of Colonial Virginia* (W. W. Norton & Company, 1975).

folks were discouraged from moving to these neighborhoods by realtors and denied loans by the banks. When a Black or Brown family looked at available homes in these areas, realtors would tell them the homes were unavailable and simultaneously approach the White neighbors and tell them the value of their homes would significantly diminish if Black or Brown people moved in.[8]

Union work and the GI Bill were how my family was able to go from working class to lower middle class to middle class. In my family, the American Dream was achievable, in part, because of societal and systemic racism. Redlining enabled my grandparents and parents to purchase homes in desirable neighborhoods and to accrue wealth through their home equity, which supported their lifestyles. The wealth that came with home ownership and union jobs created a funnel through which wealth was passed on to the next generation; it was a lot more than just hard work. My grandparents didn't want Black or Brown people in their neighborhoods because they were convinced that Black and Brown people were mostly criminals and that their presence would diminish the value of their homes, nor did they want their kids around Black and Brown people. While they were not in a Jim Crow state, they largely believed in separation and semi-equal.

---

8. Richard Rothstein, *The Color of Law: A Forgotten History of How Our Government Segregated America* (Liveright, 2017).

How can the American Dream be achievable for everyone when society requires conformity that includes bias, **discrimination**, and racism and allows only one predetermined way of existence? How can there be "liberty and justice for all" when for centuries non-White racial identities were considered less than, inherently criminal, or inherently harmful to societal status and allowed for practices such as redlining, which was in place until 1968 when the Fair Housing Act was enacted?

Very few of my family members lived in neighborhoods with racial or ethnic **diversity**, and they all believed they lived in good neighborhoods with other good people. My parents' home was on a steep, hilly, short block with only about six houses, and we lived in a small, one-story ranch-style home between two hills. No one could go anywhere when it snowed because the cars would slide down the hills and collide with each other. The neighbors diagonally across from us, the Wozniaks, had kids around the same age as my sister and me, so they were the neighbors with whom we built the closest relationships: Erling, Guadalupe, Angelica, and Olivia. Olivia was my age, and as children we spent time together every day. We colored together, learned to roller skate together, and played both board and imaginary games together.

One of the nursery rhymes we'd sing together was "Ten Little Indians." In addition to being offensive to Indigenous people, the name is also the revised version of "Ten Little Monkeys," and the original song was "Ten Little N****rs," which explored and celebrated various ways for Black boys to die and be killed. The updated version appeared in cartoons we watched, such as when Tweety Bird used the rhyme to count gunshots indicating the murder of Indigenous people. Looking back, I see we learned how to count using cartoons and a rhyming song that made light of the trauma and genocide of Indigenous and Black people, a rhyme that found glee in imagining ways to hurt, torture, and kill Black children. We also delighted in singing, "Tikki, Tikki, Tembo," a racist and made-up folklore by Westerners claiming it's based on an old Chinese folktale about how Chinese people give their children names. None of the story is true or accurate, and the song doesn't contain any real Chinese words. The book of the same name has inaccurate caricatures based on melded stereotypes of multiple Asian cultures. It's a sickening experience to realize, process, and name how many ways I learned, absorbed, and even delighted in racism without questioning it.

Olivia and I also played Cowboys and Indians. The Cowboys were always the good guys, and since we of course both wanted to be good guys, we had to take turns. When playing this game, we used my cap gun, a toy pistol with a holster and belt and a paper strip of small explosives that make a loud bang and smoke when the trigger is pulled.

We'd chase each other around our front yards pretending to shoot and kill Indigenous people. This not only normalized the genocide that occurred to Indigenous people in the country's origin story but also allowed us to have fun pretending to do the same thing.

I first asked my parents for the gun after watching the television show *Dukes of Hazzard* with them in the early- and mid-1980s. The show is an action–comedy about two cousins who were on the run from the law for distributing moonshine in Georgia. The cousins engage in all sorts of hijinks while trying to expose corrupt officials, and it made both my parents laugh, so I had positive associations with it. In addition to the gun, I also asked my parents for the manual-pedaled ride-on car version of the Dodge Charger named General Lee, a reference to General Robert E. Lee, a Confederate general during the Civil War. I loved pedaling my way around our block, up and down our street, and into the Wozniaks' driveway. My General Lee car was bright orange with a Confederate flag on the hood and "GLEE" on the license plate. I pedaled my heart out while consistently wearing a massive smile on my face. I cannot imagine how it felt for Guadalupe as she watched me pedal up to her home in my toy car.

Guadalupe was Mexican and from Texas, and her family lived there while we were neighbors. She was one of the only people I met as a child who was not from New York, Ireland, or Italy. She also spoke Spanish, which I thought was so cool, as my family had stopped speaking Italian or using any Celtic expressions to better assimilate into the US. I loved going over to Guadalupe's because she was affectionate, always had lots of snacks, and took care of me when I had bloody noses, which was a frequent occurrence in my youth. My parents told me I could spend time with her because she was a "good one." The message I took away from this was that Guadalupe and her family were the exception, embodying goodness among people who shared a common racial identity.

Obviously my family and upbringing included a lot of racism. This primary pillar of my socialization helped shape my racism; that is a fact. Unfortunately, our society doesn't allow for much nuance, complexity, or duality. I both hold the trauma I experienced in my childhood and acknowledge the intergenerational trauma patterns that harmed some of the people who hurt me. I have both fond memories of some of my elders and bad memories that acknowledge the hate they carried. Binary thinking and categorizing, like good and bad, limits our ability for authentic connection, healing, and seeing each other's full humanity.

Chapter 5

IN GOD'S SHADOW

Faith, Fear, and the Unholy Lessons of Racialized Religion

The next primary pillar of socialization in my life was our Catholic church, St. Joseph. It was under the Archdiocese of Rockville Center on Long Island, and we all received our guidance from the pope(s) of the day. Faith and religion had the most significant influence on determining good, bad, right, wrong, and evil in my family.

I separate faith and religion because I believe there are some crucial distinctions. Faith is a deeply personal and private belief system. For me, faith is believing in something bigger than myself and my fellow humans; it's believing in a divine being or beings that can offer lessons, guidance, warnings, and comfort, and in their wisdom as a source for my tutelage. Religion, by contrast, is man-made. The four largest religions are Christianity, Islam, Hinduism, and Buddhism. **Catholicism** is a branch of Christianity, along with many others, including Pentecostalism, Lutheranism, Baptist, Episcopalianism, Methodism, Protestantism, and Eastern Orthodoxy. All these denominations believe in God and Jesus, but the rules, lessons, rituals, practices, and interpretations of various scriptures vary, sometimes greatly. Religion also often has a formal and informal hierarchical organizational structure. Though faith and religion are often spoken about interchangeably, faith to me is more significant than any institution, structure, or person. While they can go hand in hand, it was essential for me to understand the distinction as I redefined what it meant to be good and a person of faith.

My parents spoke to the priests and nuns regularly for guidance and consultation on topics ranging from God's plans to which milk our family should buy, and everything in between. Rituals in our household included morning prayers, evening prayers, and bedtime prayers. We had Bible study or worship once a week, Penance once a week, and Mass once a week—unless a holiday, funeral, or special event was occurring, such as a visit from a bishop, in which case we had Mass twice a week. Jesus, Mary, Joseph, various saints, and the devil were the other invisible residents in our home. My mother called upon them regularly to support her in putting the rest of us down: "Lord, give me the strength not to kill my children. Please help them to be better people. What did I do to deserve this, Lord? Help me to understand."

Our church was almost entirely White. All the priests and nuns were White, and the visiting bishops and cardinals were White. This was true of the churches throughout our town and neighboring towns. The non-White parishioners of our church largely stayed on the periphery. They attended Mass but stayed to the side of the chapel, often toward the back, and spoke only with the priests and nuns. These fellow parishioners were asked to engage only in behind-the-scenes activities, such as preparing food for the food bank, cleaning the church during non-service times, and sewing projects for the faith leaders' robes. My exposure and engagement with these community members was limited, and this was largely by design. The priests and nuns spoke about them as if they'd been destined for hell, and they explicitly stated and implied that these parishioners were saved from that destiny because of White missionary work. My parents accepted their attendance because of the shared faith and belief in God, but because many spoke English as a second or third language, their accents made my parents uncomfortable. I was encouraged to keep them in my prayers but not interact or be alone with them. The implication was that as formerly "ungodly" people, their temptation for sinning was higher, and you didn't want them to drag you down to hell with them.

The irony is that all the stories in the Bible and about Jesus take place in various areas of the Middle East. Bethlehem is where Jesus is believed to have been born and is located in the West Bank of Palestine. As the stories go, Joseph and Mary had to flee Bethlehem with baby Jesus to escape King Herod's attempt to kill young children in Bethlehem, and they found refuge in Egypt. Jesus walked the Wadi Qelt in Palestine's West Bank on his walk between Jericho and Jerusalem in the parable of the Good Samaritan. He also crossed the River Jordan to be baptized by John the Baptist and is believed to have died in Golgotha, just outside of Jerusalem. There are also stories that took place in Syria, Turkey, Israel, and present-day Iraq. Yet all the images of Jesus, Mary, Joseph, the apostles, angels, and saints around our church depicted them as White.

Our church also shared Catholic media with us, including TV programming, movies, cartoons, and books, all portraying the Catholic characters as White. The true ethnicities and cultures of those in the Bible were minimized, denigrated, or eradicated, including Jesus'. White portrayals of religious figures helped me feel connected to Jesus, God, and the religion. God was our deity. God was our master. We considered God to be the creator of all things that have ever existed and will ever exist. We also believed he made us in his image. The implication was that if you looked more like God and God looked more like you, then not only were you likely to be closer to God than those who didn't, but anyone who didn't look as much like him was likely to be closer to the devil—and therefore closer to sin and considered dangerous.

It took around-the-clock intentionality and vigilance to stay in good standing with God and the church. Distancing ourselves from and ignoring the Black and Brown parishioners of our congregation was an easy way to avoid sin, temptation, and ending up in hell.

Even with all the spoken and unspoken rules in my youth and early adulthood, I enjoyed church and having faith. It felt comforting to have a higher being to turn to when something felt heavy, hard, scary, or confusing, and it was grounding to have a higher being to express gratitude to for large and small moments. I was grateful for the practice of humility during times of excitement, joy, or blessings. It felt reassuring never to feel alone and always have someone from whom to seek guidance. I also loved the various rituals and practices for different holidays, such as the extra songs on Christmas Eve and during special events, one on which the **Sacraments of Initiation** took place. People got dressed up, extended family attended, and we had a big party.

The Sacraments of Initiation can vary for children and adults, but as someone born into Catholicism, my first sacrament was my **baptism** as a baby. Being baptized as a baby is a practice to ensure you can get into heaven if you die before your religious studies begin. I began my religious studies, also known as the **Confraternity of Christian Doctrine** (CCD), when I entered first grade at the age of six. This practice is designed to provide religious education to children attending secular schools. As soon as that education begins, so do the preparations for the second sacrament, the Eucharist, or Holy **Communion**. Once you've gone through the second sacrament, you're allowed to receive Communion, the body and blood of Christ, during Mass services, as long as you stay in good standing with the church. In my church, the timing of Communion aligned with another sacrament, the Sacrament of Confession and Reconciliation, also known as **Penance**. Once a child reaches the Age of Discretion (or Accountability) in the Catholic Church, typically at seven years old, they're considered responsible for their own beliefs and actions. Before receiving our first Communion, we had to go to our first Confession and complete our first Penance.

Confession is a time to anonymously (or not) confess your mortal and **venial sins** to a priest. It's a space to share thoughts, behaviors, and/or actions that would disappoint God or the church, a space to unburden yourself regarding anything you feel guilty or ashamed about. The priest can absolve you of your sins and determine your Penance, which is how you can atone for the wrongs you've committed. This is essential for maintaining good standing with God and the church to be eligible for entrance into heaven upon death. Most often, Penance would include asking for forgiveness or praying and being of service to the church or others. Absolution was practically instantaneous.

At my first Confession, I felt riddled with confusion. I hadn't committed any **mortal sins** like murder or adultery, but I did have some questions. I'd tried to join the church's Catholic youth athletics baseball team for a few years and was told I couldn't join because I was a girl. When I asked whether there was a girls' baseball team, I was informed that there was—it was called softball, and that league was only for girls fourteen and older. Father Casper and I had a circular conversation in the confessional:

"Why can't I play baseball?" I asked.

"Because you're a girl, my child," he gently proclaimed.

"That doesn't make any sense. I know how to play baseball. I play with the boys sometimes, and I'm pretty good," I persisted.

"I bet you are, my child, I bet you are," he said with an amused tone.

"So why can't I play?" I asked, confused.

"Because you are a girl," he restated, and round and round we went.

We ended with a prayer, and he absolved me of my sins. My Penance was fifty "Our Fathers" and ten "Hail Marys." I liked the idea of having a private space to unburden myself of anything I felt guilty about and being instantly forgiven, but my first Confession left me feeling confused and *less than*. I had no idea about **misogyny** or **patriarchy**.

Another component of the Holy Communion ceremony is for boys and girls to walk slowly on opposite sides of the middle aisle, their heads tilted down with their eyes looking at the ground and their hands clasped in a prayer position in front of their chests. This was done both to demonstrate the anguish Jesus's followers felt after the crucifixion and to remind us of our humility in receiving the sacrament. We practiced this for over three months at our CCD classes.

The attire for our first Holy Communion was rooted in a long-standing tradition within the church: Boys wore black suits, and girls wore white dresses resembling a traditional wedding dress, complete with a white veil, white ankle socks, a white Communion purse, and white dress shoes. The reason for this was that the first Communion equated to marrying God. I went back to Confession for guidance. I did not want to wear a wedding dress, and I did not feel ready for marriage.

Father Casper smiled at me with his warm smile as he invited me into the open room of the confessional. "What is weighing on you, my child?"

"Forgive me, Father, I'm not ready for marriage. And I don't want to wear a wedding dress." Immediately, I began to sob.

Leaning toward me, he handed me a tissue and said, "I see. I see. Let's take these one at a time. Are you scared for your first Communion?"

"Yes, if it means I have to be married!" I exclaimed. Up to this point in my young life, family members, other parents, churchgoers, and other adults regularly asked me who I wanted to marry. They'd ask whether there was a boy I liked, who I thought my husband would be, and how many kids I wanted to have with my husband. I often responded that I didn't want a husband or kids, and they'd chuckle at me and tell me I'd change my mind.

Attempting to reassure me, Father Casper said, "Oh, my child. My sweet child. It's not like how your parents are married. It's more akin to committing yourself to God. And you love God, yes?"

Feeling unheard, confused, and depleted, I inquired, "So why do I have to wear a wedding dress?"

He simply stated, "It's tradition and part of the ceremony."

We ended with a prayer, and he absolved me of my sins of doubting God's will and the church's teachings. My Penance was to write out "God loves me. I love God. It is easy to commit to God" fifty times and say more prayers.

At home, I protested, telling my parents I did not want to wear a bridal dress or marry God. They were aghast. "You have to go through Communion. It's a sacrament. You'd be going against God." The statement "going against God" was weighty. I felt guilty for feeling the way I did, and I was ashamed and embarrassed to disappoint my parents and Father Casper. I also didn't want to be a disappointment to God. I felt vulnerable and exposed, as though I were wearing a see-through wet coat.

A lot of bargaining took place. First I prayed and talked to God. I told him I was committed to him but was not going to marry him, that my heart wasn't going to do that part. I wasn't going to say any of the words or prayers during the ceremony, either. Second, I stated in my CCD class that I didn't want to wear a dress, and I told my parents I wanted to wear the suit the boys were wearing. That was too much. My parents were upset that I'd exposed this embarrassing desire within the church community, and Father Casper and Sister Eileen were horrified and in disbelief that I didn't want to marry God or wear a wedding dress. No one was interested in my protest. The adults discussed what to do in a whisper with each other, without involving me; they didn't want me to speak, so it was challenging to communicate with them. They told me my outbursts and behavior were embarrassing and disappointing to them, that I was going to go through with Communion to be accepted into heaven, and that they wouldn't let me drag the whole family down to hell because I refused to honor God.

It was a lot of pressure. I felt as if the heavens might open up and God himself might come down to smite me. I wanted to be a good Catholic, but I was struggling. My heart, soul, and mind believed in God and Catholic teachings, but my body wasn't aligned. My body was in a constant state of panic, as if I were hanging onto the edge of a cliff, clawing my way back up. I didn't understand why God didn't want me to play baseball. I didn't understand why I needed to confess all my sins to a priest once a week, even when I didn't have anything to share. I didn't understand why my love and devotion to God were in doubt because I didn't want to wear a dress, and I didn't understand why people always asked about my future husband. I felt confused because everyone in my family was Catholic and never seemed to question the church or God. Ultimately, I didn't want to disappoint them or be the cause of my entire family going to hell, condemning them to an eternity of torture, pain, and suffering after death, so I completed my second sacrament.

The practice of weekly Confession with Penance from seven years old until my mid-twenties convinced me that I was inherently not good and always making mistakes and causing harm to those around me. I worried that with all the mistakes I was making and all the harm I was causing, in the end I likely wouldn't go to heaven, and I worried I was going to go to hell because, after all, God was always watching. Committed to showing God that I was good enough to be able to go to heaven, I thought one way I could demonstrate this, following my rebellious outbursts, was to provide greater service to the church and its priests during services. One of my favorite parts about Mass services was the beginning, when gifts (the Bible, blood, and bread of

Christ, and incense) were walked up to the altar from the back of the church with the priests, brothers, altar boys, and ministers. It was considered divinely special and an honor to be the family or person chosen to serve in this way during a service.

My mother always felt that we needed to bring up the gifts at least once a month to demonstrate our devotion to God, our goodness within the church, and our goodness toward the other churchgoers. For a church with thousands of parishioners, this was a significant challenge that pained my mother deeply. In my opinion, this goal of hers stemmed from her need to convince herself of her goodness, and she projected it onto our family. To ease her pain and demonstrate my commitment to our faith, my family, and the community, I approached Father Casper and Father Tony after Mass one day to become a faith volunteer.

"Excuse me, Fathers," I said as I approached with reverence and humility.

"Oh my, child. There is determination written all over your face," Father Tony quipped.

"Yes, Father." At age ten, I stood in front of these two men who towered over me in their clean and pressed white robes, each wearing beautiful green and gold sashes draped around their necks.

Father Casper invited me to share: "What is this important business you'd like to discuss with us, sweet child?"

"Well, Fathers, I would like to show my love to God by becoming an altar boy." I imagined the pride my mother would feel watching me be of service in this way during Mass. I hoped it would show her my goodness and help her feel assured of her goodness, both as a person and as a mother. Bad kids were not altar boys, and bad moms did not have kids who were altar boys.

The Fathers were baffled at my request. The surprise showed on their faces as they looked at each other and then down at me. Kneeling so his face would be closer to mine, Father Casper said, "My child. It is so beautiful that you want to express your love to God in even greater ways. There are several ways to do that. You can help Sister Eileen prepare the refreshments following Mass or help Sister Margaret pick up any bulletins that fall in the parking lot. Or if you'd like, you could lint roll the confessionals to prepare them for reconciliation." Both Fathers smiled and nodded their heads. They seemed relieved not to have to address my request directly while still offering me options to serve.

I tilted my head to the side and looked at them through the corner of my eye, trying to avoid being disrespectful. "Fathers, forgive me; I already do those things. I want to be an altar boy." I felt nervous because it was a serious no-no to question the priests or the church.

Father Tony walked away, and Father Casper placed his hands on my shoulders as he began to stand up. "Sweet child, you can't be an altar boy. You're a girl," he said quietly so as not to disrupt the other conversations around us. "Girls can't be altar boys." In his right hand were rosary beads, which he moved in front of my chest, raised above my head, and used to draw an invisible cross from right to left across my face before finally kissing them and raising them to God. He then patted my head and walked away.

I was stunned and confused. I didn't quite understand what had just happened. Both priests had greeted me warmly, and when I shared what I wanted and how I could serve, they offered the often-ignored, unseen, and thankless work I was already doing. That would not help repair the damage I'd caused by my rebellion.

As a child, I overall felt confident in my relationship with God. I prayed and spoke with him every day, often multiple times. He was my best friend, and I trusted him with everything. The confusion I experienced was often rooted in the rules, messaging, and practices within our church. I sat in the pews every Sunday, reading along in the Bible as our priests led Mass and delivered their homilies, interpretations of the readings from the Bible. Homilies were lessons that were always woven into present-day events, issues, or the current societal discourse. I often found myself looking down at the Bible and reading the words written there, then lifting my head toward the priest, thinking that his homily didn't quite match the lesson I was taking from the story in the Bible.

Throughout my years of religious study, I engaged in various forms of service to embody many of the lessons shared in the Bible. These were the moments when I felt closest to God, and I wanted to be a good representation of him here on Earth. We primarily focused on embodying the following teachings:

- "Do everything in love" (1 Corinthians 16:14).[9]
- "Love is patient, love is kind. It does not envy, it does not boast, it is not proud. It does not dishonor others, it is not self-seeking, it is not easily angered, it keeps no record of wrong. Love does not delight in evil but rejoices with the truth. It always protects, always trusts, always hopes, always perseveres. Love never fails. But where there are prophecies, they will cease; where there are tongues, they will be stilled; where there is knowledge, it will pass away" (1 Corinthians 13:4–8).
- "Love one another as I have loved you" (John 13:34).
- "Do to others as you would have them do to you" (Luke 6:31).

We also often volunteered at food banks and served meals at programs for the elderly, individuals with limited resources, and those experiencing being houseless.

---

9. All Bible quotations are from the New International Version (NIV).

We visited with community members who were homebound for a variety of reasons, such as being in hospice or having limited mobility and transportation options. I became pen pals with a Lance Corporal in the Marine Corps during the Gulf War of the early 1990s after our youth group had mailed thank-you cards to his platoon. These activities felt like putting our beliefs of caring for others, especially those suffering or struggling, into practice. When I heard homilies that included such topics as rising crime, theft of food from the church pantry, and the harsh punishments God and man would hand out, it felt out of line with our stated beliefs of God's messages. I secretly wondered why, if people were hungry, we would punish them for wanting to eat outside of Wednesday's meal program from 4 p.m. to 6 p.m. My tensions and confusion started to amplify.

The Ten Commandments anchor Catholicism. This includes the Commandment that "Thou shalt not steal," but why would God or Jesus not want the sick, elderly, poor, or anyone in need to eat when there was an abundance of food available? That felt unclear to me. And when the AIDS epidemic of the 1980s and '90s was killing tens of thousands of people, particularly gay men and in brutalizing ways, our church said this was God's punishment of homosexuals and they deserved the suffering they were experiencing, and our priests exclaimed this was God's wrath to eradicate the abomination of homosexuality. I felt scared, sad, and shocked as I sat receiving this message in weekly Mass. We were taught that God is love, Jesus is compassionate, and caring for those in need is a vital component of our humanity, and part of what I understood about being Catholic was caring for those otherwise discarded by society.

In 1984, Ryan White, a thirteen-year-old hemophiliac, was diagnosed with AIDS following a blood transfusion. I saw myself in him as soon as I saw him on TV. When his school was trying to prevent him from attending and his local community was bullying and discriminating against him, I kept thinking Jesus would be his friend, so I wanted to be his friend. I even wrote him letters—secretly, of course. However, our priests had us pray for his fellow community members not to get AIDS from him. This made me feel queasy in my body, but I never said anything to anyone because I didn't want to get in trouble.

My favorite older cousin was gay. He was very affectionate in a way none of my other family members were, warm and present when he engaged with me. He always danced with me at family parties, and his smile made me smile. After he tested positive, my family stopped inviting him to family events because of "his deviancy." When he did attend a family event, the adults would scurry around the room warning all the children. I was told not to hug him, not to let him kiss my cheek or hand, and to get out of the pool if he went in and then take an immediate shower.

A few of my older uncles died of AIDS, and 95 percent of our family decided not to hold or attend their funerals. We didn't even admit that those uncles were gay. Funerals were a big deal for my family; they were days long and featured numerous gatherings, food, booze, prayers, and religious services. I knew my heterosexual family members felt afraid of this new disease, but it felt cruel to belittle and ostracize people who were scared or suffering, especially in their deaths. It felt like the exact opposite of what Jesus would do.

When I was in middle school, the AIDS quilt came to our school and covered the entire gymnasium floor, extending up onto the bleachers and stage. Each square represented someone lost to the AIDS crisis, and each was designed and constructed by the people who loved them. Most of the squares had someone's name on them, and many displayed the year the person was born and the year they died, with most individuals passing away under the age of forty. Some of the squares had fabric flowers sewn into them; some had song lyrics of peace, love, and grief; and others had quotes about acceptance, resistance, and humanity. The gymnasium was silent the entire time as people moved around the room absorbing the magnitude of what the quilt represented. Most of the people remembered in the quilt were being remembered by their chosen family and friends. Too many of their families and religions, like mine, had disavowed and discarded them.

The quiet weight of that gymnasium, of lives judged, discarded, or erased, lingered long after I walked out. In my own home, that same pressure to conform and be "saved" showed up early, beginning when I was twelve and my mother and Aunt Mara called me into the kitchen for a conversation I knew wouldn't be good. I'd just come home from school and was heading to my room when I heard my mother say in a low, deep tone, "Casey. Come here, please." My stomach turned, as I recognized the terseness of her words.

I took a deep breath as I turned into the kitchen entryway. The kitchen was small and clearly designed in the 1970s, with brown and orange flower petals that looked like bubbles covering the walls. My mother firmly told me to sit down, then pointed to the chair that was turned sideways so that I could sit there and see both her and my aunt as they stood in front of the stove to speak to me. To keep it light, my aunt pretended to give me a hard time for not hugging her or giving her a kiss hello; I was required to provide hugs and kisses to all family members upon greetings and farewells.

Aunt Mara laid it on thick: "What am I, chopped liver?! You can't say hello to your aunt who wiped your ass as a baby?" An obligatory and lackadaisical hug and hello followed, then silence ensued. My mother pointed to the kitchen chair, once again directing me to sit. I knew this meant I was at least in for a stern talking-to about something. I just hoped it would be quick.

After my mother and aunt exchanged a glance, my mother finally said, "We are worried about your soul. We worry you're going to do something really stupid, like choose to be a faggot."

I was taken aback and confused by the formality of the conversation. I didn't know what they were talking about and felt entirely surprised by these opening statements. I also felt scared of what was about to happen and wondered whether they were going to send me away, whether they'd beat it out of me, and whether they'd had this conversation with my sister. Totally unsure of how I was supposed to engage in this conversation, I just said, "Okay."

My mother continued: "I mean it. Under no circumstances are you allowed to be a faggot! You'll go to hell." My aunt nodded along as my mother drove her point home. The threat of hell was significant. My mother went on to say, "Nobody will love you. You won't be able to be a part of this family anymore. You'll be alone, and God will hate you, too." My aunt chimed in to add that I would get AIDS, die alone, and go to hell, and they both reaffirmed that if I chose this for myself, no one would come to my funeral or even care when I died. I believed them. I'd been watching my family and my church condemn and ostracize people for years.

I felt frozen and could barely breathe. I knew what that derogatory term meant because many family members called my cousin that behind his back. Despite most of the adults in my life constantly asking me questions about marriage and kids, I didn't think about boys or girls very much at this stage of my youth. My mother's mental health and the secrets we held to protect her from being seen as "crazy," and thereby ostracized, consumed most of my mental and energetic space.

As I sat in that kitchen chair absorbing all the terrible things that would happen to me if I weren't straight, I debated in my head:

If God is love and God made everyone, wouldn't God love gay people?

No, homosexuality is a sin, and sinners burn in hell.

But if you confess that you're gay, aren't you absolved from your sins?

Not this one.

But God loves all and everything.

Except gays, non-Catholics, people who get divorced, people who have or support abortion, people who don't believe in God, people who don't come to Mass on Sundays, people who don't pay the appropriate tithe, people who murder, people who lie, people who are envious of others, people who question God, people who take advantage of the poor, people who defraud others of their wages ... it's a slippery slope!

Okay, no being gay.

My mother and aunt had this conversation with me two more times during my adolescence.

I was committed to being a good Catholic, a good child, and a good person. I felt the pressure to be good at home, at church, at school, in activities, at work, and in all my relationships. I didn't want to go to purgatory or hell, and I didn't want to cause anyone I loved to go there either. And I absolutely did not want to be kicked out of the family due to my queerness, gayness, or lack of goodness, nor did I want to lose my family or my church or make God hate me. So I committed to and leaned into my relationship with God and the Catholic Church, continuing my religious studies and going through my next sacrament of initiation, **Confirmation**.

I was in ninth grade at the time, and once you go through Confirmation, your intensified religious education can cease. With this ending, I lost one of the ways I could prove myself to my family and to God. I craved that structure. I felt the need to prove to my family that I was good and would not take them to hell, so I joined two Bible studies that each met once a week. We talked about scriptures, how they applied to current events and pop culture, and of course what Jesus would do navigating all the issues of the day. When I arrived at college, I even became a Catholic campus minister to ensure I maintained my devotion to God and demonstrated my commitment to him and to others.

I was operating from a place of fear—fear of disappointing God and my family, and fear of going to hell. I felt panicked over what I could and could not say and whether I could ask questions, and I was overwhelmed by all the things I was supposed to do to be seen as a good person: help my parents and contribute labor and money to my family; support the church with time, labor, and money; get good grades; and help my community members by volunteering. I was exhausted doing everything I was told to do and drained by always feeling like I had to say yes to requests. Feeling burdened by all these demands, I was often quite cranky and one of the most uptight peer ministers. I didn't take time to chitchat or small talk because I thought only lazy people did that. I was an ardent rule follower in public and expected that behavior from everyone else.

I was in between tasks when Daniel, one of my fellow peer ministers, asked me whether I was "family" while we were sitting in the ministry office. I asked him what his last name was since interactions like this happened frequently in my large family, and he answered, "No, baby, are you f-a-m-i-l-y?" as his mannerisms became more animated. I had no idea what he was talking about. Then he invited me to join him and a number of other ministers for drinks. I was stunned because I wasn't as cool as they were, but I was also excited because they were all older students, which made me feel like I belonged in that space.

A few days later, we met at the ministry office after hours. Almost everyone who worked for the Catholic campus minister program was there, and they were all dressed up in bright colors, boas, and glitter. I pretended I didn't notice as I walked up in my gray T-shirt, jeans, and Adidas sneakers. One of my peers had the keys to the van and we all piled in. There almost wasn't enough space; people were on each other's laps, and I sat on the floor. About thirty minutes later, we pulled up to a dark, poorly lit building that looked like an old, defunct bar. I didn't see anyone else around. Daniel huddled everyone up before instructing us to follow him, while everyone else was giggling, sipping from a flask, and beginning to dance around. He then brought us to the back of the building, where a very muscular woman in leather was monitoring the door. Externally, I like to think I was looking unfazed by the secrecy and excitement of others, but internally, my whole self was screaming and wanting to run away.

As each person entered the space, the music got louder, and the sounds of joy reverberated out the door. They'd brought me to a gay bar.

I tugged on the arm of another minister, Tina, and asked her, "Are we at a gay bar?"

As the smile on her face grew, she exclaimed, "Yes, we are! And we come every Thursday!"

I was dumbfounded, and now my external expression matched my internal feelings. My jaw hung open as my knees went weak. "What about going to hell? Aren't you afraid of that?" I whimpered.

Tina wrapped her arm around my shoulder, pulled me closer into her, and asked, "First time? You'll be alright. Stay close to me. Oh, and to answer your question, no, I am not afraid of going to hell. I'm a wonderful person and a whole lot kinder than some of the folks who are certain they're going to heaven. Come on, let's dance."

Tina was kind. Daniel was, too. This experience allowed me to begin discovering the differences between my faith and my religion. My religion told me to be quiet, ignored and dismissed my questions, and told me because of my assigned gender at birth I was incapable of doing many things in this life. My religion required me to be obedient and to feel guilt and shame in who I was as a human as a regular practice, and it instilled the fear of God and hell inside of me at a cellular level. My faith, on the other hand, supported my ability to care for others and to reflect on the moments of the day. Later, my faith encouraged me to be accountable to myself and to others, and it helped me understand the importance of making amends when harm did occur. My faith helped me to stay grounded and grateful, in good times and bad, and it bolstered my resilience and ability to be steadfast in the face of adversity.

My faith is rooted in love, kindness, and our collective humanity.

Chapter 6

THE CURRICULUM OF COMPLIANCE

How School Shaped My Understanding
of History, Power, and People

The next pillar of my socialization was public school. The schools near our home were almost entirely filled with White students, and I attended a smaller-sized school with fewer than thirty students per class. Many teachers also had their own children enrolled, which created a sense of closeness even as the culture remained narrow. My high school principal had once been a priest and had also been my father's principal. I started kindergarten in 1983 and graduated from high school in 1996, receiving what many considered a "good education" in a well-resourced Long Island district.

Thanks to strong unions such as the New York State United Teachers, our classrooms remained small and our teachers well-supported. Most teachers genuinely cared. Yet state mandates, parental influence, and standardized testing demands restricted the curriculum. We memorized facts, rehearsed dates, and celebrated figures deemed "foundational" without ever learning who was missing from the story. I absorbed cultural norms and power structures not just through lessons but through the rhythms of school life. Popularity depended on conventional attractiveness, wealth, and athleticism. "Goths" were feared, "invisibles" ignored, and the "troublemakers" often presumed guilty of any anomalies to the desired experience. I learned early on that social survival meant being alert, agreeable, and never asking the kinds of questions that could make others uncomfortable.

In primary school, many of the activities we participated in weren't designed for critical thinking or intellectual engagement. Instead, they carried subliminal cultural messages that reinforced dominant narratives. Around major holidays, we were expected to complete teacher-prescribed arts and crafts, including making mock eagle feather headdresses for Thanksgiving. We paraded through the hallways, tapping our mouths with open palms to mimic what we thought were "Native" sounds. We were never taught that in many Indigenous cultures, the eagle feather headdress is sacred, something earned through acts of leadership and honor. What was sacred to others became costume and play for us, divorced from any real context or reverence.

The same lack of historical accuracy and cultural awareness extended into our music education. Students were required to either learn an instrument or join the choir. I chose choir, since my mother dedicated my time outside of school to dance. Twice a year, we performed songs that were considered "traditional" and uncontroversial. But those songs—"Turkey in the Straw," "Oh Susanna," and "Dixie Land"—were deeply embedded in the legacy of American minstrel shows. They were popularized through blackface performances that dehumanized and mocked Black people, often portraying them as ignorant or inferior for White audiences' entertainment.[10] The fact that we performed these songs without context or conversation about their origins showed how thoroughly school settings sanitized these cultural artifacts. Even the ice cream truck jingle, which still plays "Turkey in the Straw," carries with it this history of racial caricature, though no one ever taught us that.

Bias didn't stop at music class; it shaped our extracurriculars too. My principal banned the musical *Grease*, claiming it promoted promiscuity among girls, but he approved *Oklahoma!*, a story that erases the violent colonization of Indigenous land. He rejected *Les Misérables* for its themes of rebellion but greenlit *Miss Saigon*, a production steeped in racialized stereotypes and the sexual exploitation of

---

10. "Blackface: The Birth of an American Stereotype," Smithsonian Institution | National Museum of African American History and Culture, accessed June 14, 2024, https://nmaahc.si.edu/explore/stories/blackface-birth-american-stereotype.

Asian women. These decisions signaled which narratives were considered respectable, which were dangerous, and whose stories were worthy of school-wide attention.

In the classroom, particularly in history lessons, we were taught from a single perspective. The teaching style mirrored the Drama Triangle: Every story had a hero, a victim, and a villain.[11] There was only one version of the truth, one set of facts, one correct answer. We didn't analyze events from multiple viewpoints or ask who the narrative left out, nor did we learn how to think critically about power, perspective, or consequences. Instead, we memorized predetermined dates and stories designed to cultivate certainty rather than inquiry. The same stories were recycled year after year, shaping our understanding of American history as linear, moral, and resolved.

Still, there were exceptions. My eighth and tenth grade history teacher, Mr. Agosti, broke away from rote memorization. He was young, animated, and scruffy, often teased by the older office staff for his appearance, but he had a gift for making history come alive. He wrote songs about historical figures, turned lessons into plays, and encouraged us to debate and ask questions. His methods sparked my interest in learning. Yet even in his classroom, we faced limitations.

---

11. "The Drama Triangle," Leone Centre Team, Psychotherapy Resources, December 27, 2022, https://psychotherapyresources.com/discover/relationship-counselling/drama-triangle/.

Our school had almost no racial diversity, and although discussions around gender and socioeconomic differences occasionally surfaced, we never deeply explored them. Without a variety of lived experiences in the room, even the best-intentioned conversations remained surface-level.

From kindergarten through high school, I excelled at memorizing facts and dates. That skill helped me test well and earn As and Bs in history, reinforcing the illusion that I knew the topic. My teachers praised me, my parents celebrated my report cards, and I came to believe that knowing the answers meant knowing the truth. It wasn't until years later that I realized how little of US history I'd actually learned—and how much had been deliberately left out. For nearly twenty-five years, I've been unlearning and relearning history, reconstructing what I was taught alongside the realities I was never shown. Unlike the immersive nature of school, this reeducation competes with work, home, and daily responsibilities. Learning now is slower, fragmented, and often more difficult. Still, it's necessary. This ongoing practice of un/relearning is not just about correcting facts; it's about understanding how narratives shape identity, justify power, and obscure harm.

The history I was taught had a very clear author: those who conquered. My early lessons framed colonizers as heroes and Indigenous people as "savage," "hostile," and "uncivilized." These narratives positioned White Europeans as victims or benevolent figures and taught me to align my values with their version of events. There was no mention of European imperialism, genocide, or land theft. Instead, the focus was on exploration, settlement, and the supposed bravery of people seeking "freedom." We were never taught that land is power, how its ownership allows people to grow food, build homes, and influence culture. We didn't learn that acquiring land meant displacing others, nor that land theft was foundational to American wealth. I wasn't taught that 90–95 percent of the Indigenous population perished following European arrival, nor that many of those deaths were due to diseases spread by colonizers who lacked basic hygiene practices.[12] Instead of reckoning with the loss of Indigenous life and culture, we made construction-paper headdresses and celebrated Thanksgiving.

The framing of slavery furthered erasure. I learned that slavery happened in the South, and that the North, abolitionist and righteous, fought to end it. Abraham Lincoln was cast as the great liberator, the Civil War as a moral battle. Missing were the complexities. Northern resistance to war was often rooted in apathy, not solidarity. Many Northern White men didn't feel compelled to fight in a war to liberate Black people because they didn't see it as

---

12. Roxanne Dunbar-Ortiz, *The Indigenous Peoples' History of the United States* (Beacon Press, 2015).

their issue. Lincoln initially refused to enlist Black soldiers; only later, out of necessity, did he change his position. I never learned about the labor strikes and pay inequities Black soldiers endured during the war, such as the eighteen-month protest for equal pay waged by Black Union soldiers who continued to fight even while their wages were withheld. It wasn't until 1864, under mounting pressure, that Congress finally granted them retroactive equal compensation.[13] That story never made it into my textbooks. I learned simplified, sanitized stories meant to uphold national pride and maintain the status quo. I was shielded from the truth that slavery was a nationwide economic engine, that systemic racism was built into our laws, and that the American story, as I learned it, was one of omission.

I was taught that after the Civil War, America redeemed itself, that Reconstruction was a period of justice and repair, that the Thirteenth, Fourteenth, and Fifteenth Amendments righted the wrongs of slavery. I memorized their definitions, including the abolition of slavery, the guarantee of citizenship, and the extension of voting rights to Black men. The message was clear: America had addressed one of its greatest sins.

---

13. "African-American Soldiers During the Civil War," *U.S. History Primary Source Timeline: Civil War and Reconstruction, 1861–1877,* Library of Congress, Classroom Materials, accessed June 1, 2024, https://www.loc.gov/classroom-materials/united-states-history-primary-source-timeline/civil-war-and-reconstruction-1861-1877/african-american-soldiers-during-the-civil-war/.

But what I wasn't taught was the fine print.

No one told me that the Thirteenth Amendment includes the loophole "except as a punishment for crime," nor that this loophole would be used to justify the forced labor of incarcerated people—mostly Black and Brown—well into the present day.[14] I didn't learn about prison labor or how corporations and governments profit from paying incarcerated people cents per hour, if at all. I didn't know that entire industries, from agriculture to manufacturing to firefighting, depend on this labor,[15] nor that the system was designed, not broken.

The Fourteenth Amendment sounded like a promise: equal protection under the law. But I wasn't taught that it took almost another hundred years and countless civil rights battles before that promise came close to being honored. And even then, the backlash began immediately. No one told me that our country has a distinct pattern of progress being followed by resistance, that when we feel threatened or afraid we strip others of their rights under the guise of safety. I didn't learn how that fear was weaponized, how the War on Drugs,

---

14. Michelle Alexander, *The New Jim Crow: Mass Incarceration in the Age of Colorblindness* (The New Press, 2010); Nazgol Ghandnoosh, "One in Five: Ending Racial Inequity in Incarceration," The Sentencing Project, October 11, 2023, https://www.sentencingproject.org/reports/one-in-five-ending-racial-inequity-in-incarceration/.

15. "Captive Labor: Exploitation of Incarcerated Workers," American Civil Liberties Union (ACLU), June 15, 2022, https://www.aclu.org/news/human-rights/captive-labor-exploitation-of-incarcerated-workers.

officially declared in 1971, was used to target Communities of Color under the pretense of public safety.[16] I didn't know then that long before Nixon, drug laws criminalized Chinese immigrants, Mexican Americans, and Black communities, and that hysteria and propaganda were tools, not just reactions. I never learned that Nixon's advisors admitted years later that their goal was to disrupt Black organizing and silence antiwar voices, not to protect anyone from harm.

When it came to the Fifteenth Amendment, I learned that Black men could vote, but I wasn't taught how quickly and brutally poll taxes, literacy tests, threats of violence, and acts of violence undermined that right. I wasn't taught how voter suppression didn't end but just evolved, and I didn't hear about the modern tools with old intentions, such as voter ID laws, polling site closures, or purges of voter rolls. It took years before I understood how rights could be given on paper and denied in practice.

I also didn't learn how language itself carries the legacy of oppression. I grew up saying things like "cakewalk," "master bedroom," "holding down the fort," and "peanut gallery" without knowing their origins. These phrases, so ordinary and unexamined, were born from systems of enslavement, segregation, and genocide. "Cakewalk," for example, began

---

16. "Nixon Adviser Admits War on Drugs Was Designed to Criminalize Black People," Equal Justice Initiative, March 25, 2016, https://eji.org/news/nixon-war-on-drugs-designed-to-criminalize-black-people/.

as a dance enslaved people used to mock their enslavers as an act of resistance; it was later co-opted by those enslavers. "Brown bag" refers to tests used to exclude people with darker skin tones from opportunities. I used these words casually, unconsciously. When I was first called out about them, I froze, shocked by my own ignorance.

Even holidays held hidden truths. I grew up celebrating the Fourth of July as our great national liberation story. We waved flags, grilled burgers, and set off fireworks. I didn't know there was another day—Juneteenth—that told a more complete story of freedom. I didn't learn that slavery continued even after Abraham Lincoln signed the Emancipation Proclamation in 1863 because Confederate states rejected his authority, nor did I know that the Proclamation meant nothing in the territories still under Confederate control and that that freedom only became real when Union soldiers arrived and enforced it. I didn't know that Galveston, Texas was the last place to receive that news, two and a half years later on June 19, 1865. I didn't learn about Juneteenth until adulthood. I never knew it was a Black celebration of liberation, a domestic Independence Day that had been buried by a country that prefers fireworks and flag-waving over reckoning and remembrance.[17]

----

17. "The Historical Legacy of Juneteenth," Smithsonian Institution | National Museum of African American History and Culture, accessed June 16, 2024, https://nmaahc.si.edu/explore/stories/historical-legacy-juneteenth.

The Compromise of 1877, the quiet political deal that ended Reconstruction and began the erasure of Black political power,[18] was something else I never knew about. I didn't learn how quickly Jim Crow laws followed nor how they codified segregation, upheld **White supremacy**, and shut Black people out of institutions they'd barely begun to access. Religion was used to justify these hierarchies, with White pastors preaching divine segregation, and I didn't see it, nor did I see how newspapers, posters, and pulpits portrayed Black people as criminals and savages to justify systems of exclusion and violence. I didn't learn that policing was designed to enforce those portrayals and preemptively treat Black people as threats while White violence went ignored. I never heard about the Ku Klux Klan, the Red Shirts, or the White League in school, much less how their terror campaigns were met with silence or even support from White communities.[19] The message I absorbed was that racism was personal, not institutional, individual, not organized. Racism surrounded me whether I knew it or not.

18. "The Compromise of 1877, a Story," African American Registry, accessed June 15, 2024, https://aaregistry.org/story/the-compromise-of-1877-a-short-story/.

19. W. E. B. Du Bois, *Black Reconstruction in America: An Essay Toward a History of the Part Which Black Folk Played in the Attempt to Reconstruct Democracy in America, 1860–1880* (Harcourt, Brace and Company, 1935).

Coded Language Examples

"Blacklisted"

Though not originally about race, the term reinforces the association of "black" with something negative or undesirable, echoing broader Western associations of blackness with badness, which can contribute to implicit racial bias.

"Brown bag"

The "brown paper bag test" was used within some Black communities in the early - to mid- 20th century to determine privilege or access based on skin tone. If a person's skin was darker than a brown paper bag, they might be denied entrance to certain institutions or social groups.

"Eeny, meeny, miny, moe…"

Older versions of this rhyme in the US included a racial slur instead of "tiger" in the second line ("catch a ___ by the toe"). The offensive version persisted into the 20th century, especially in the American South.

"Holding down the fort"

The phrase has roots in US military frontier days and can evoke the history of colonization and the defense of settlements from Native Americans, potentially minimizing or erasing the violent context of westward expansion.

"Long time, no see"

This is a grammatically incorrect English phrase that likely originated as a mock imitation of Indigenous or Chinese speech patterns, reflecting a history of mocking or demeaning non-native English speakers.

"Master bedroom"

The term linked to the era of slavery in the US, with "master" evoking plantation hierarchies. While the term more likely arose in early- to mid- 20th century real estate marketing, the association has led many real estate professionals to favor alternatives such as "primary bedroom."

"Peanut gallery"

In vaudeville-era theaters, the "peanut gallery" often referred to the segregated section where Black patrons sat. Thus, using the phrase can evoke a class- and race-based hierarchy of worth or taste.

"Thug"

In modern Western usage, particularly in the US, "thug" has become a racially coded term disproportionately applied to Black men, often as a euphemism for "criminal," "dangerous," and "unworthy."

"Powwow"

The term trivializes the spiritual and cultural significance of actual powwows to Indigenous communities.

"White glove service"

The term carries associations of racial and class privilege, particularly when service roles were historically filled by people of color serving white elites.

Figure 2

Just as glaring as what I wasn't taught about harm was what I wasn't taught about brilliance. I didn't learn that Black and Brown inventors shaped the world I live in. No one told me about Judy Woodford Reed, the first Black woman to receive a US patent, or Sarah Elisabeth Goode, who designed the foldaway bed. I didn't learn about Sarah Boone's ironing board innovation or Garrett Morgan's traffic signal, and there was no mention of Marie Van Brittin Brown, who cocreated the first home security system, nor Lewis Latimer, whose carbon filament made light bulbs last. I didn't learn that Indigenous people invented syringes, goggles, and rubber long before Europeans arrived, nor that colonizers would later take credit, like Charles Goodyear did once he vulcanized rubber.[20] My education erased not just the horrors of the past, but the genius too.

Exclusion was also embedded in law, yet no one mentioned the Chinese Exclusion Act of 1882 or that Congress extended it in 1892 and made it permanent in 1902. I didn't know that tens of thousands of Chinese workers built the Transcontinental Railroad under grueling conditions, working longer hours for lower pay and having to cover their own food costs, that at one point 90 percent of railroad

---

20. Thomas H. Maugh II, "Mayas Mastered Rubber Long Before Goodyear," *Los Angeles Times*, May 31, 2010, https://www.latimes.com/archives/la-xpm-2010-may-31-la-sci-rubber-20100531-story.html.

laborers were Chinese immigrants, nor that the country thanked them with a ban on their existence.[21]

America constructed a racial hierarchy where White, Christian, land-owning men sat at the top and Chinese, Black, Mexican, and Indigenous people were forced to the bottom, and I didn't know it. Nor did I learn that when the US needed China as an ally during World War II, the Chinese Exclusion Act was finally repealed, but with a quota: Only 105 Chinese immigrants were allowed per year.[22] And while those doors were just starting to open, new ones were slammed shut. Executive Order 9066, for example, authorized the forced removal of Japanese Americans—citizens included—from their homes after Pearl Harbor, and families were given as little as forty-eight hours to pack what they could and report to "relocation stations." Over 120,000 people, most of them citizens, were sent to remote internment camps across the country. They lost homes, businesses, savings, and years of their lives, and most were never charged with a crime. We never talked about any of this,

---

21. "Chinese Railroad Workers in North America Project at Stanford University," Chinese Railroad Workers in North America Project announcement, August 31, 2020, https://web.stanford.edu/group/chineserailroad/cgi-bin/website/.

22. "Repeal of the Chinese Exclusion Act, 1943," United States Department of State | Office of the Historian, Milestones: 1937–1945, accessed July 10, 2024, https://history.state.gov/milestones/1937-1945/chinese-exclusion-act-repeal.

nor how the government made only symbolic gestures in return. It wasn't until much later that I learned about the Japanese American Evacuation Claims Act of 1948, which offered only partial compensation,[23] and no one ever taught me that while Japanese Americans were rounded up en masse, only a handful of German and Italian Americans were incarcerated.[24] The difference wasn't lost on me once I finally saw it: again, race determined who was feared and who was forgiven.

The Japanese American community lost an estimated $1.3 billion in property and $2.7 billion in income during the years of forced internment. I didn't learn that in school. I didn't learn about the congressional investigation decades later, nor that it took until the 1980s for the US government to formally acknowledge the injustice. Between 1984 and 1988, a series of laws were passed that offered a $20,000 payment to each surviving person who'd been incarcerated, but by then, many had already died. No one

---

23. National Archives, *Executive Order 9066: Resulting in Japanese-American Incarceration (1942)*, Milestone Documents, accessed July 11, 2024, https://www.archives.gov/milestone-documents/ executive-order-9066.

24. Alan Rosenfeld, "German and Italian Detainees," *Densho Encyclopedia*, accessed July 11, 2024, https://encyclopedia.densho.org/ German%20and%20Italian%20detainees/.

mentioned how long justice took or how small it was when it arrived.[25]

I also didn't learn how thoroughly American history had erased women's voices, especially the voices of Women of Color. That erasure felt deliberate. In school, there was barely a mention of how the law once treated women not as people but as property. In 1769, the Blackstone Commentaries declared a woman's legal existence effectively suspended within marriage, and by 1777, every state had passed laws stripping women of the right to vote—laws that remained in place for nearly a century and a half.[26] I never learned any of this.

When we studied the Nineteenth Amendment, I heard about Elizabeth Cady Stanton, Susan B. Anthony, and Lucretia Mott. Their names were etched into my understanding of suffrage. But I didn't learn about Sojourner Truth, the formerly enslaved woman who spoke truth to power and fought for the liberation of all women, not just White ones. I didn't learn about Ida B. Wells, who fearlessly documented

25. T. A. Frail, "The Injustice of Japanese-American Internment Camps Resonates Strongly to This day," *Smithsonian Magazine*, January 2017, https://www.smithsonianmag.com/history/injustice-japanese-americans-internment-camps-resonates-strongly-180961422/.

26. "Timeline of Legal History of Women in the United States," National Women's History Alliance, accessed July 12, 2024, https://nationalwomenshistoryalliance.org/resources/womens-rights-movement/detailed-timeline/.

the horrors of lynching and challenged the racism within the suffrage movement itself, and no one told me about Mary Church Terrell, a founder of the NAACP who worked tirelessly to uplift Black communities through education and advocacy. Mississippi refused to ratify the Nineteenth Amendment until 1984, the year after I entered kindergarten, yet I never knew, nor that the struggle for voting rights didn't end in 1920. It just changed shape.

Growing up on Long Island during the 1980s and '90s did offer me one very unique educational experience. Every year, Holocaust survivors who were the grandparents and relatives of my classmates visited our classes to share their traumas, their stories, and the lessons they hoped we would learn. Every time a survivor entered our classroom, the classmate whose relative it was would introduce them. It felt intimate to be a part of their family of origin's storytelling, to witness the pain of the weight of those stories, and to be invited to never let that happen again—to anyone.

I remember Bubbe Esther vividly. She came to my class in elementary school, middle school, and high school. She was very petite, always wore sweaters and big, thick glasses, and carried handkerchiefs she'd made at home. She spoke so softly that you needed to lean in as she spoke in order to hear, and she had a beautiful laugh that occasionally slipped out and surprised her. She shared her story about being a young girl when Hitler first came into power and how her parents tried to reassure her that they'd be okay. She shared how different things felt when the hateful words coming through the radio began presenting in her neighborhood, in the apartment building in which she and her family lived, and at school. It started, she said, with the way people would look at her and her family, and later it transitioned to people spitting and cursing at her and her family. She named how confusing and scary it was that people in positions of authority ignored or joined in on the torment and how places that had been safe, fun, and connective, such as neighborhood parks, the local grocery, and school, became intimidating and dangerous. Her father was beaten up a number of times on his way to work as a baker. She cried as she reflected on the anguish of that period and her loved ones who were lost.

Bubbe Esther's anger always presented itself when she talked about the anti-Semitic propaganda that pervaded Germany. Her voice would crack at the disorientation around how little it took for friends, neighbors, and fellow Germans to move from being in community together to viewing her and her family as less than human. She told us the story of when her father received the cloth Stars of David and brought them to her mother to sew onto their jackets. Neither of her parents could muster a word, and she and her two younger brothers sat together on the floor, also speechless. Her next memory of that moment is her mother sobbing into each of her children's jackets.

It wasn't long after this moment that Nazi soldiers took Bubbe Esther's family. When they were first arrested, she shared, they clung to each other as they were shoved around, screamed at, and processed. At fourteen years old, she was pulled from her family's arms and sent to Ravensbrück. For years after the war ended, she didn't know where her family was sent or whether they survived. Only one of her younger brothers did. She showed us the prison number tattoo she received on her left arm and invited us to use two of our fingers to feel it. The first time I touched her tattooed concentration camp number, it felt like touching the ghost of a memory. I felt transported to the reality of the time, a heaviness in my body that I'd never felt before, and a deep sadness for her immeasurable pain that I can still feel when I think of Bubbe Esther.

Before she'd leave our classroom, she'd encourage us to always ask ourselves whether we were operating from fear and hate or from love and peace. She exclaimed that fear, hate, ignorance, and bias made it possible for the Holocaust to occur, and she encouraged us to question stories about people told by those other than themselves. The last message she wanted us to receive was to interrupt cruelness, meanness, and bullying. I don't think I truly understood the power of her storytelling and lessons back then, but I reflect on them now with immense gratitude.

Among all the other things I never learned was that the US largely wanted to stay out of World War II and joined only because of the attack on Pearl Harbor. When we did join the war, we were the heroes, the victors, the good guys. It wasn't until much later that I discovered a more complex history of that time. In *Mein Kampf,* for instance, Hitler praises the US for its efforts to prioritize **White Supremacy Culture** and legalize a racial hierarchy, and US race laws served as the foundation for the Nuremberg Laws. The only German critique of US race laws was that they didn't go far enough. In his 2017 book *Hitler's American Model: The United States and the Making of Nazi Race Law,* James Q. Whitman illustrates how racism has been embedded into US law throughout US history. Those laws allowed German lawyers to explore and write their own laws to legally discriminate, disenfranchise, and abuse the Jewish people. Hitler also praised the US's slaughter of Indigenous people as something to admire and learn from.

A group founded in 1940 called the America First Committee, led by individuals with anti-Semitic views and pro-fascist ideologies, was a prominent voice of students, FDR-haters, pacifists, and others against war in general that pressured the US to stay out of WWII. Two outspoken celebrities in leadership positions on that committee included

Henry Ford and Charles Lindbergh. Henry Ford was a rabid racist and anti-Semite who wrote a book entitled *The International Jew: The World's Foremost Problem* in 1922. In it, he openly rallies against jazz music, blaming it as the cause of "America's moral decay." He was so against jazz music that he poured money into bringing square dancing back into mainstream culture. He even gave millions of dollars to schools to make it a part of their gym classes and hosted lavish square-dancing events throughout the US. I learned to square dance in middle school because of Ford's robust, continued investment into schools. Not ironically, Ford blamed the Jews for jazz music even though jazz was created by Black communities in New Orleans in the late nineteenth and early twentieth centuries.[27] And in 1940, referring to Charles Lindbergh, also an anti-Semite and a suspected Nazi sympathizer, Ford told the FBI, "When Charles comes out here, we only talk about the Jews."[28] These two men were celebrated in my history books, and my classmates and I were encouraged to admire and revere them.

---

27. Jonathan R. Logsdon, "Power, Ignorance, and Anti-Semitism: Henry Ford and His War on Jews," Hanover College History Department, accessed July 12, 2024, https://history.hanover.edu/hhr/99/hhr99_2.html.

28. John J. Dunphy, "Charles Lindbergh: Aviator and Extremist," Medium, January 27, 2019, https://johnjdunphy.medium.com/charles-lindbergh-aviator-and-extremist-bdcce12fccbd.

Rosa Parks and Dr. Martin Luther King Jr.'s legacies were included in my education, but they were reduced to singular messages. Dr. King was a man of God who led people through their faith and civil unrest to achieve greater societal equity by ending the Jim Crow laws of the South. Rosa Parks was a strong, faithful, and kind older woman who refused to give up her seat on a segregated bus. One message I received was that Dr. King and Ms. Parks were good people because they were civilly disobedient. The Black Panthers, as I was taught, were violent and dangerous because they were not as civil or obedient, and they carried guns and wore black leather and sunglasses.

Our school hung MLK posters with quotes like these:

- "I have a dream that my four little children will one day live in a nation where they will not be judged by the color of their skin but by the content of their character."
- "I have decided to stick with love. Hate is too great a burden to bear."
- "Let no man pull you so low as to hate him."

It was only later I learned he also said:

- "A riot is the language of the unheard."
- "True peace is not merely the absence of tension; it is the presence of justice."

- "Whenever you take a stand for truth and justice, you are liable to scorn."

I also didn't learn until later about all the positive community programs that the Black Panthers led and the impact they had on those they served, including developing community survival programs to support Black people and other minoritized communities. These programs provided free food for anyone in the community in need, such as free breakfast for children before school to support their ability to learn throughout the day. They also provided free medical services to those with health needs, a lack of access to health-care, and medical mistrust, as well as free community and health education, including reading and writing programs. The weapons and self-defense trainings helped keep their communities safe from police brutality.[29]

One consequence of not learning multidimensional and nuanced history is that it made it harder for me to comprehend other people's realities that differed from my own. It made me resist the thought that what I learned might not be true or accurate, and it challenged my self-perceptions of being smart, informed, and a good person.

---

29. "Black Panther Party's Community Survival Programs 1967–1982," Black Panther Party Alumni Legacy Network, accessed July 14, 2024, https://bppaln.org/programs.

I didn't like school, but I loved learning. My schooling often required sitting still, being quiet, listening to learn, studying at home to absorb, and taking tests to demonstrate comprehension. It felt boring and robotic, but it worked— I not only absorbed the narratives told to me without question but embraced and embodied them.

Reflecting on my education, I now understand how much was hidden beneath the surface of what I was taught, how many truths were buried beneath sanitized stories and one-dimensional narratives. The history I absorbed was not neutral. It was carefully curated to preserve a sense of national pride, to protect **Whiteness**, and to perpetuate the illusion of **meritocracy**. What I once took as fact was often propaganda dressed up as curriculum.

Coming to terms with that has been both liberating and sobering. It has called me into a lifelong practice of questioning and curiosity, and that practice has called me to greater responsibility. It requires me to seek out the stories of suppressed voices and narratives. I will never stop learning. I will never stop asking, "Whose story is missing?" My freedom is bound up in the truth—and in everyone else's liberation, too.

Racialized Realities in the US

We live in a highly racialized society. In other words, race matters.

This is evident across data about life outcomes related to racial advantage and disadvantage economic, health/life expectancy, education, criminal justice, housing, and more.

We're all part of the picture. It is not possible to live in US society and not experience the impacts of structural racism (unearned advantage or unearned disadvantage) in our lives.

None of us asked for this. None of us are responsible for the past, but all of us are responsible for the present and, to some extent, the future.

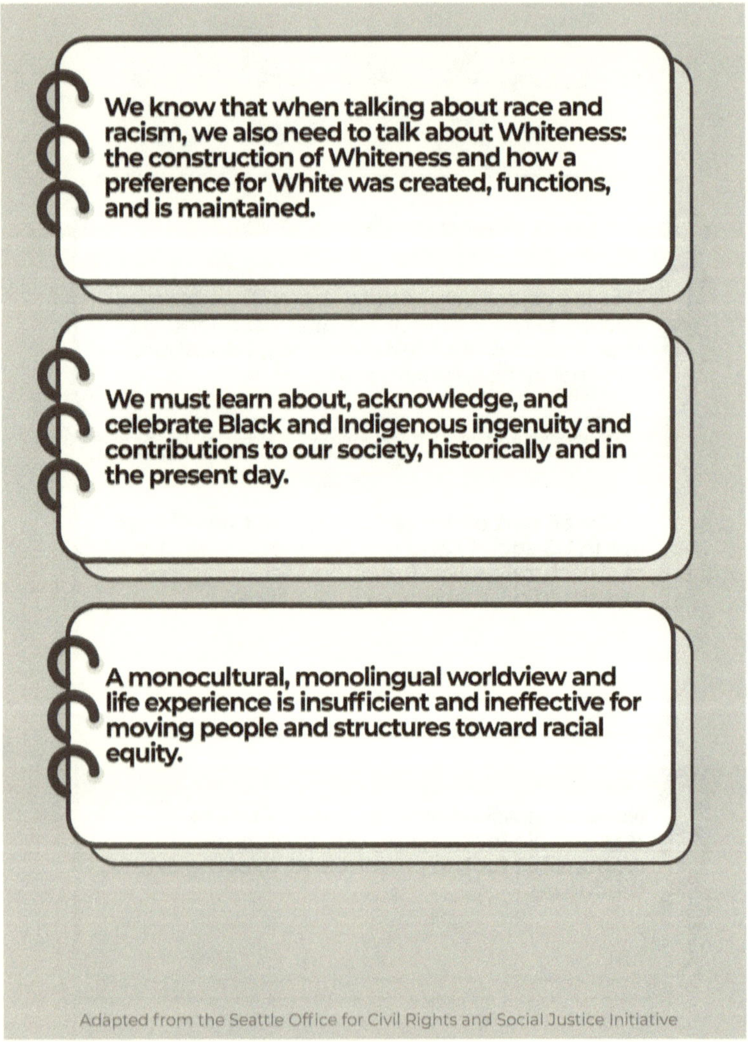

We know that when talking about race and racism, we also need to talk about Whiteness: the construction of Whiteness and how a preference for White was created, functions, and is maintained.

We must learn about, acknowledge, and celebrate Black and Indigenous ingenuity and contributions to our society, historically and in the present day.

A monocultural, monolingual worldview and life experience is insufficient and ineffective for moving people and structures toward racial equity.

Adapted from the Seattle Office for Civil Rights and Social Justice Initiative

Figure 3

Chapter 7

POP CULTURE, POLITICS, AND PROGRAMMING

Media, Memory, and the Making of My Mind

The 1980s was a decade marked by seismic cultural shifts and transformative global events that redefined politics, identity, and social consciousness across the world. As Cold War tensions simmered and technological innovations surged, nations grappled with uprisings, assassinations, and protests that challenged existing power structures. From the devastating AIDS epidemic and the nuclear arms race to anti-apartheid activism and rising racialized violence in the US, the decade revealed deep societal fault lines and sparked resistance across continents. The fall of the Berlin Wall, the Tiananmen Square massacre, and the emergence of influential social movements captured the spirit of a world in transition—one where media, music, and grass-roots mobilizations became tools for resistance and expressions of hope.

This timeline explores the pivotal events of the 1980s, inviting reflection on how these moments shaped the narratives, fears, and possibilities of a generation.[30]

TIMELINE OF MAJOR EVENTS THAT SHAPED MY SOCIAL DEVELOPMENT IN THE 1980S

This timeline illustrates just some of the violence that has gone on in our past and still affects us today, primarily because we too often treat things as a "one-offs" and people as "bad individuals" without ever acknowledging the ongoing cultural components such as racism, sexism, and homophobia. I invite you to reflect on how these moments shaped the narratives, fears, and possibilities of a generation.

Extended

- Nuclear arms race and protests (1945–1990)
- Cold War (1945–1991)
- South African Apartheid (1948–1993)
- Vietnam War (1955–1975)
- Eritrea's War for Independence (1961–1993)
- Nicaraguan Revolution (1960s–1990)
- Northern Ireland Conflict (1968–1998)
- Lebanese Civil War (1975–1990)

---

30. Data taken from a variety of sources; see appendix B for a more comprehensive timeline.

- Operation Litani, Israel invades Lebanon (1978–1982)
- Angolan Civil War (1975–2002)
- Iran Hostage Crisis (1979–1981)
- Soviet–Afghan War (1979–1989)
- Iran–Iraq War (1980–1988)
- South Lebanon War and South Lebanon Conflict (1982–2000)
- First Intifada (Palestinian uprising against Israel in Gaza and the West Bank) (1987–1993)
- Second Intifada (Palestinian uprising against Israel in Gaza and the West Bank) (2000–2005)

1980

- China's population reaches one billion; China creates the One Child Policy.
- The Miami Riots follow the acquittal of White police officers in the brutal beating and killing of Arthur McDuffie, a Black man, during a traffic stop.

1981

- Global recession.
- Pope John Paul II is shot in an attempted assassination.
- The CDC publishes its first official report on GRID, later known as the AIDS virus.
- Egyptian President Anwar Sadat is assassinated.
- Assassination attempt of Ronald Reagan.

1982

- Vincent Chin, a Chinese American man, is brutally beaten to death by two White autoworkers who blamed Asian Americans for the decline of the US auto industry; despite the murder being racially motivated, the perpetrators receive no jail time, sparking nationwide protests and mobilizing the modern Asian American Civil Rights Movement.
- Three abortion clinics are bombed in Washington, DC, in a coordinated attack by right-wing extremists.

1983

- Darryl Gates, a Black man, is severely beaten by LAPD officers during a traffic stop, highlighting growing racial tensions between Black communities and police in Los Angeles.
- The US invades Granada.
- The left-wing group Armed Resistance Unit bombs the US Senate, protesting US foreign policies.

1984

- Eleanor Bumpurs, a sixty-six-year-old Black woman, is shot and killed by NYPD officers during an eviction, after which she became a symbol of excessive force against Black citizens.
- Indira Gandhi, India's prime minister, is assassinated.

- Charles Howard, a gay man, is attacked, thrown off a bridge, and murdered in Maine by three teenagers.
- Firebombing attack at the Feminist Women's Health Center in Florida.
- Radio host Alan Berg is assassinated in Colorado by right-wing White supremacist group The Order for speaking out against anti-Semitism and White supremacy.

1985

- The Philadelphia Police Department bombs a Black separatist group location, MOVE, killing eleven people and destroying sixty-one homes.
- White supremacist Patrick Purdy opens fire at Cleveland Elementary School in California, killing five children and injuring thirty-two others.

1986

- Space Shuttle *Challenger* explodes with teacher Christa McAuliffe on board.
- The Iran–Contra Affair is exposed.
- The People Power Revolution ousts Philippines Prime Minister Ferdinand Marco.
- Swedish Prime Minister Olof Palme is assassinated.
- An Idaho-based White supremacist group commits an arson attack on Temple Beth Shalom in Washington State.

- The explosion at the Chernobyl Nuclear Power Plant scatters radioactive materials across Europe.
- White Christian nationalists bomb five abortion clinics in Florida, Georgia, and Tennessee.

1987

- Terry Waite, a special envoy for the Anglican Church, is kidnapped in Beirut and held until 1991.
- Burkina Faso President Thomas Sankara is assassinated.
- The trial of Nikolaus "Klaus" Barbie, the Nazi "Butcher of Lyon," begins in France.
- Ronald Reagan visits West Berlin and challenges Mikhail Gorbachev to "tear down this wall," referring to the Berlin Wall erected in 1961 as a part of the Cold War.
- A gunman takes forty-one people hostage at a Korean American-owned electronics store in California, ranting about his hatred for Asian immigrants.
- Former Nazi Rudolf Hess commits suicide in a German prison.

1988

- The USS Vincennes shoots down the passenger plane Iran Airlines Flight 655, mistaking it for an F-14 Tomcat, killing all 290 aboard.
- Osama bin Laden forms Al Qaeda.

- Al Qaeda assassinates Afghan Taliban resistance leader Ahmad Shah Massoud.
- The Iran–Iraq war ends with an estimated death toll of more than one million people.
- Mulugeta Seraw, an Ethiopian immigrant, is beaten to death by White supremacists in Oregon.
- White supremacist Richard Lee Snell opens fire at a gay bar in Pennsylvania, injuring several patrons.
- Pan Am Flight 103 explodes in Lockerbie, Scotland, killing 259 on board and eleven people on the ground; a Libyan intelligence officer is convicted of the attack.

1989

- Japanese Emperor Hirohito dies, ending a sixty-two-year reign.
- The Exxon Valdez oil spill taints hundreds of miles of Alaskan coastline.
- Students march through Beijing to Tiananmen Square, calling for a more democratic government; after a few months of peaceful and increasing protests, Chinese troops fire on civilians, killing an unknown number of people in the Tiananmen Square Massacre.
- Yvonne Smallwood, a Black woman, is shot and killed by NYPD officers under controversial circumstances, sparking community outrage.

- An arson attack occurs on the Upstairs Lounge, a memorial honoring the thirty-two patrons killed and fifteen patrons injured during the 1973 Upstairs Lounge Fire.
- The Berlin Wall falls.
- US troops invade Panama.
- Leonard Kravitz is stabbed in New York by a group of White supremacist skinheads.
- An arson attack destroys an abortion clinic in Virginia.
- The Central Park Five (later known as the Exonerated Five), five Black and Latino teenagers falsely accused of rape and vilified with racist rhetoric in the media, are arrested, sparking Central Park protests.

As if all that weren't enough, movies, television shows, news programs, and significant global events were other pillars of socialization that shaped me. These media forms both expanded my worldview and embedded me with coded racialized language. As a child I was obsessed with watching reruns of the television show *Good Times*, a show about the Evans family of five living in a public housing project in Chicago, their dynamics, and Black activism of the 1970s. In one episode, their child neighbor Penny, played by a young Janet Jackson, reveals the abuse she's been experiencing at the hands of her mother. The Evans are kind to Penny, ask her about what's happening at home, listen to her, and believe her. You could feel their desire to protect her through the screen. Watching the characters love each other, fight with each other, disagree with each other, navigate racism together, and laugh together offered me a glimpse of what kind of love was possible in a family. The Evans help Penny navigate the situation, and she's ultimately adopted by their neighbor Willona, who's a strong, loving, caring, and stylish woman. Witnessing Willona care for Penny was the first time I realized the love, care, and relationship I desired most in the world did not have to come from a biological relative. Watching these episodes was also the first time I learned that what was happening to me by my mother was not okay. The show felt like a lifeline and a hug at the same time. Television was a staple of my childhood.

This was also the Ronald Reagan era with persistent use of the term "welfare queen," a derogatory term used to describe individuals perceived to misuse or abuse federal welfare programs. Ads including the term almost always showed an image of a Black woman in a Cadillac either smiling or laughing. Ronald Reagan was also intensifying his War on Drugs by prioritizing punishment over treatment, and his policies led to a massive increase in incarceration rates for nonviolent offenses.

I reflect often on what was going on nationally, culturally, and in my family throughout my lifetime. For example, I was born three years after the Vietnam War ended, during the

Cold War, and around a year before the Iranian Hostage Crisis took place. I remember hearing the relief from my family, within our church, and on the news that the Vietnam War had ended, accompanied by grief over the 58,000 soldiers who'd died and the 300,000 reported wounded. Many of the families who lost a loved one in Vietnam also experienced familial losses in World War II. My grandfather Hermit would have me feel the shrapnel remaining on the left side of his head and along the outer part of his left leg. Feeling the pieces of metal that remained under his skin always made me feel a little queasy. I didn't like feeling such hard pieces of various sized metal on so much of his body. He was proud of his service—we all were—I just wished he hadn't come home so beaten up. His eldest son, my uncle, served in Vietnam. He wasn't around much, he didn't talk much when he was around, and I never saw him without at least one bottle of booze on his person. The only thing my family ever said about him was that only a shell of him returned from the war.

At church, we prayed for those still healing, for those serving at the time, and for peace. As a part of my religious studies at church, I put food bags together to be delivered to struggling veterans and made cards for service members, always understanding with heaviness that WWIII could break out at any time. In those moments of service and prayer, I felt both connected to something larger than myself and constantly on edge while absorbing the message that danger was always just beyond the horizon. And that sense of looming threat didn't stay confined to church. It seeped into the stories I was told at home, at school, and in the media I consumed. The world was presented to me through a lens of heroes and enemies, good guys and bad guys, and I clung to those narratives to make sense of the fear surrounding us.

At the same time, I learned that the US and the Soviet Union (Union of Soviet Socialist Republics, or USSR) teamed up to fight Hitler in WWII and afterward were enemies. We were the good guys, and they were, of course, the "bad commie bastards." My father loved action movies, so when he was home on the weekends, we went to the theater. Communism, the KGB, and Soviet spies were common themes and main components within the storylines of the 1980s movies we saw. *Red Dawn* (1984), for instance, is a worrisome and enticing tale in which the USSR invades the US and a scrappy group of good-looking young people fight back through subterfuge and mischief.

There was also *Rocky IV* in 1985, in which 1980s perpetual underdog Sylvester Stallone as Rocky had to fight USSR-sponsored Ivan Drago, a highly celebrated (when he wins) government-sponsored sports star. The movie mirrored the fact that the US and USSR competed together in most world events, including the Olympics, unless either was hosting it. When they did compete against each other, regardless of the sport, it always felt like we needed to cheer and root for

Team USA and boo the Soviets. Watching *Rocky IV* helped my father and I maintain an Olympic spirit between the 1984 and 1988 Olympics. We even chanted "U-S-A!" while watching the movie at home. At school, we practiced fire drills in case of a fire emergency and nuclear drills in case the Soviet Union attacked. I knew nothing about geopolitics or how power functioned, but I absorbed the message that Russians or members of the Soviet Union were dangerous and not to be trusted. At the same time, 1980s movies also offered rogue Soviet spies who would help Americans, depicting them as "the good ones."

Other movies in this decade, including *Revenge of the Nerds*, *Police Academy*, *Ghostbusters*, *Back to the Future*, *Porky's*, *Sixteen Candles*, *The Breakfast Club*, and many others, passed along various forms of sexual assault for humor. These movies portrayed sexual assault victims as people—mostly women—who couldn't take a joke, or worse, who were ultimately grateful to their perpetrator for the experience. I learned to expect sexual harassment and assault as a normal part of life. I also learned that if I did experience sexual assault, the first question I'd be asked was, "What did you do to lead the person on or ask for it?"

My sister was a teenager in the late 1980s and early '90s. Because she was my big sister, I thought she was the coolest and wanted to be just like her. As soon as she'd get home from school, she'd turn on the TV to MTV. I remember the firestorm of panic that overtook national and local news when MTV debuted in 1981 with "Video Killed the Radio Star." Many of the adults in my life believed MTV was destroying the youth of America, making us lazy, promoting promiscuity, and letting people think they could have self-expression outside of what had been prescribed to them by societal rules. Fear-based messages of societal collapse abounded. The rhetoric and panic created tension between my parents and my sister, and my parents, teachers, priests, and extended family members exhaustedly repeated politicians' talking points: "This music will rot your brain," "This music encourages girls to be sluts," "This music makes you think gangs and drugs are cool." The policing of the content, language, and topics discussed in music and movies became so intensified that there were senate and congressional hearings to discuss what was happening and what to do about it.

Regardless, my sister plastered her walls with torn-out magazine photos and posters of INXS, Bon Jovi, Guns N' Roses, and Aerosmith. Mixed in were pictures of the male teen heartthrobs of the day, including Johnny Depp, River Phoenix, and Leonardo DiCaprio. They served as a visual protest to our parents' rejection of these "bad influences" on her impressionable mind. I wanted to mimic my sister and have an answer when adults asked me who I wanted to marry or wanted as my husband, so I also hung photos. I cut out photos of Ronald Reagan from the newspaper and posted his pictures on my wall. He was the president, and there were framed photos of him (from his acting days) hanging in the bathroom at our church. I thought I'd come up with the perfect crush to deal with the adult inquiries of my relationship status, and it made me feel more like my big sister.

Since I did not yet have an understanding of coded language or economics, when Reagan used the term "welfare queen," I thought it was hilarious. The fact that welfare queen caricatures were common fodder on sitcoms and sketch comedy shows reinforced my initial reaction. As a child, I thought having our own economic system, "Reaganomics," was also an indication of being smart and a big deal. My father was a part of the Professional Air Traffic Controllers Organization union strike and was fired by my first crush.

As I reflect, the 1980s and '90s weren't just a backdrop to my childhood but were active participants in shaping my beliefs. The Cold War loomed, and the threat of nuclear devastation was a constant undercurrent. White Christian nationalists bombed and attacked abortion clinics across the country, and politicians, faith leaders, and media figures used culture wars to stir fear, turning immigrants, artists, and entire genres of music into scapegoats. People like my family—immigrants who'd once fled horrors of their own—were now framed as the ones taking jobs from "real" Americans.

As a teenager, I heard that rap music, Black women in R&B, and video games were destroying society. These weren't new messages; they echoed the same tired rhetoric used against jazz, rock 'n' roll, and other movements that pushed against the mainstream. It was fear disguised as morality, control masquerading as concern. And even when I didn't understand the full implications, I was soaking it in. We all were, as evident by the common messages we received about music:

MUSIC (1920S–PRESENT) AND THE RHETORIC AGAINST MUSIC OF THE TIMES

GENRE	TIME PERIOD & EXAMPLES	MESSAGES AGAINST GENRE
Jazz	Early 1910s–1930s Billie Holiday, Miles Davis	Devil's music, trash, poison to the mind, promotes sexual deviancy, demise of the social fabric
Rock 'n' Roll	1950s Chuck Berry, Elvis, Chubby Checker, Fats Domino, Ricky Nelson	Troubling, disturbing, corrupt, diseased, vulgar, promotes promiscuity
Pop	1960s–1970s The Beatles, The Rolling Stones, The Who, The Kinks, Dusty Springfield	Devilish, corrupts the youth of America, instigates hysteria, blasphemous
Hair Metal Bands	1980s INXS, Bon Jovi, Guns N' Roses, Aerosmith	Satanic, gender-bending, morally decays young people, promotes sex, graphic

GENRE	TIME PERIOD & EXAMPLES	MESSAGES AGAINST GENRE
Rap	1990s Lil' Kim, Missy Elliot, NWA, Wu-Tang Clan	Promotes violence and thuggery, too sexual, corrupts the youth
Hip-Hop	2000s–2010s Jay-Z, Kanye West, Common, Ludacris, 50 Cent, Lil' Wayne, Kendrick Lamar, Nicki Minaj, Travis Scott, Young Thug, A$AP Rocky	Promotes drugs and violence, objectifies women

Growing up in the 1980s and '90s also meant witnessing a cascade of global and domestic upheavals: the AIDS crisis, the fall of the Berlin Wall, the end of apartheid, the collapse of the Soviet Union, the first World Trade Center bombing, the Oklahoma City bombing, and the frenzy of Y2K. These events brought waves of fear, sorrow, celebration, and confusion—all shaped by the cultural lens I was given. These years were not peaceful, and the social conditioning reflected that turbulence. Yet through it all, a dominant narrative remained: The US is the best, the US is the global moral compass, and we have to protect that morality through conformity and obedience.

Looking back, I can see how the overt and covert messages I absorbed throughout my developmental years were meticulously crafted to support assimilation into the dominant culture. These messages weren't just lessons; they were warnings. They taught me that safety, goodness, and belonging came through conformity, through aligning with societal norms without question. To deviate was to risk being labeled as bad, wrong, or dangerous. The underlying cultural narrative was clear: Challenge the status quo and you will be othered. This message echoed everywhere, from the nightly news and our Sunday homilies to classroom discussions and dinner-table conversations. Teachers framed obedience as patriotic, priests cloaked it in righteousness, and my family passed these messages down as though our salvation depended on them. I wasn't taught how to think critically or to consider multiple perspectives. I was taught how to survive in a system that demands silence, sameness, and submission.

If we remain uncritical, we will find ourselves repeating history's mistakes—repackaged and retold but rooted in the same fear-based rhetoric that shaped us. The work now is to unlearn, to question, and to reimagine what belonging can mean when it's not tied to conformity.

Chapter 8

WHAT THE F*CK DID I ABSORB?!

Reconciling Love, Harm, and Misguidance

I have a lot of gratitude for my pillars of socialization. I wouldn't be who I am today without them. Life, people, institutions, and society are all complex and nuanced, and acknowledging that does not equate to diminishing their value. My pillars also caused me harm and limited my understanding of myself, my humanity, and our society.

None of us is always right or always wrong. None of us is always good or always bad. None of us is always, if ever, perfect, no matter how we may strive to achieve perfection in the various aspects of our lives. We may desire to simplify the meanings of good and bad, right and wrong, and perfect and imperfect, but by doing so we deny our lived realities. This practice encourages us to mask our authentic selves, causes us to hide what we think others will judge us for, and promotes denying our complex individual and collective realities, and we suffer as a consequence. When who we are is incongruent with the identity and role others have predetermined for us, it fractures our souls. Feeling the need to perform or be perceived in a certain way can nurture feelings of shame and fear. These feelings often cultivate self-loathing or self-doubt, and they can manifest in excessive criticism of self or others, creating a disconnect with our own and others' humanity.

In the previous chapters, I broke down various forms of socialization I experienced individually, but the reality is that all those pillars were intersecting at the same time. Many of the messages I absorbed from these forms of socialization both reinforced and conflicted with each other, including covert and overt racist messages, along with the message that neither our current society nor our family was racist. Many of the lessons adults preached—apologizing when you've hurt someone or taking accountability for harm, whether real or perceived—often weren't practiced by those same adults.

My pillars taught me many messages about being good, some of which I still hold onto dearly, such as being loyal to the ones I love, practicing gratitude, and the importance of learning. Other vital messages and behaviors I learned from my grandmother and the church were to be generous with my spirit, time, and resources, giving them to those who have less than me, those who are hurting, and those who need a little help. Those messages and behaviors are still personal values I keep close. A mindset I had to release, however, was that these behaviors made me good, kind, or better than other people. I had to release judgments about other people's worthiness and value based on their circumstances, characteristics, or societally constructed identities. My mindset is now rooted in seeing and caring for our collective humanity.

A behavior I had to adjust was using judgment, shame, fear, and guilt to act in a way that made me feel most comfortable. For example, it was common in my family to be relentlessly pressured to engage in an act of kindness, such as taking the neighbor's trash out or visiting an elderly relative, then to take or be given credit for being such a good person. That was a lie. I never wanted to do half the things I was asked to do, but I was always happy to take compliments or credit. My mother would berate me nonstop until I agreed to the request and then share news of its completion widely with others to get credit for raising me. It was an insincere practice.

Growing up, I learned the importance of connection and community. I loved being part of a big family, as well as being connected to so many people who lived in our neighborhood, town, and the tri-state area. The idea of being on this journey together felt nourishing. That's still true, but what has changed is the need for my chosen family and community to be homogeneous. I was raised with people who looked like me and in a community that shared the same thoughts and beliefs. Now my chosen family and communities are a kaleidoscope of experiences and perspectives. We share the values of kindness and compassion and of respect and communal care. We're connected by our shared humanity, both individual and collective, making our survival inter-connected. We do not operate in a hierarchy, nor do we hoard resources. We love, support, and care for each other. We do not judge or shame one another. We challenge and support each other when we witness self-judgment occurring.

I also had to release my shame around holding onto and hiding secrets cultivated by societal stigmas. I had to understand and accept that no matter the good intentions my pillars might have had in shaping me to become a good person, a good Catholic, and a good member of society, they raised me with racism and a racist ideology.

My Uncle Enzo and Aunt Lucia, who brought so much light and laughter into my childhood, were generous with their affection, quick with a joke, and always made me feel seen and cherished. And yet it was through them that I was first introduced to a wide range of racial stereotypes and slurs, passed along not with malice but as normalized truths in the world they inhabited and helped shape for me. Those two facts are accurate, and it's a painful reality to acknowledge and accept. When I was relying on binary thinking, I couldn't consider both facts being true, so I resisted the possibility of the truth that challenged me most: that my family was racist.

My parents used racial slurs and told racist jokes in our home, but they told me never to repeat them outside the home. They also told me racism was bad and that we weren't racist because we lived in New York and knew a few Black and Brown people (maybe four), but they also referred to those people as the "good ones." And my extended family referred to Black and Brown people as animals and criminals. When we watched the nightly news, any time there was a Black or Brown person suspected of a crime, they were presumed guilty and described in dehumanizing ways. I learned these messages in my childhood home and carried them with me as I entered adulthood. I believed I wasn't racist while also laughing at racist jokes because they were just jokes and crossing the street if a Black or Brown man was on the sidewalk with me.

As I was about to start college, multiple family members told me not to date an "N" word and that I was never to bring one home with me or I'd be kicked out of the family. Given all the years of covert and overt racism I witnessed in my family throughout my childhood and young adulthood, I never questioned it. I never spoke up. I never pushed back. There were many times when I felt uncomfortable with the language and behaviors I heard and witnessed, but I did nothing.

There are plenty of reasons I can offer myself to excuse my silence and complacency, including "I was just a kid," "I didn't know better," and "Things were different back then."

But those excuses don't provide the complete picture. I felt the racism in my body; it felt heavy and made me sad. But I was also used to it. It became familiar to me because it was a part of my family. It was also in the news, even without the explicitly racist language of the generation before mine. I didn't learn much about Black or Brown history, Black or Brown excellence, or Black or Brown achievements outside of sports. I also didn't try to. Two behaviors I developed were staying silent in conversations about race and racism and relying only on what I'd been taught about US history and historical racism.

Most of the people in my socialization pillars were White. White men stood as the only historical heroes, with all their transgressions erased from the history books. The history of all minoritized identities was either entirely erased or reduced to a paltry paragraph in my schoolbooks, and standardized testing encouraged memorization and absorption of false and incomplete narratives. Jesus, a Middle Eastern man, was depicted as White in my church, and in most TV shows of the day; the White folks, particularly men, were the good guys; and everyone else was either a victim or a villain. This encouraged the development of an unconscious racial and gender hierarchy in my mind. White men were the smartest, bravest, and most trustworthy. White women were safe but also delicate, fragile, and in constant need of rescuing. Light-skinned Black and Brown individuals were often accepted, especially if they excelled in the arts or sports. Asian people were okay because they were viewed as intelligent, except if the men were hourly workers or didn't speak perfect English; then they became caricatures and the butt of jokes. Asian women were sexualized, fetishized, and silent, and light-skinned Latine[31] people were considered beautiful, especially if they entertained audiences through music and dance. Indigenous folks were presumed to exist only on reservations, and Indigenous men were a threat while Indigenous women were commonly sexualized and fetishized. Black men were dangerous, not to be trusted, and scary, and Black women were uneducated, loud, and abused social programs.

Growing up in the 1980s and '90s was both similar to and different from growing up in other generations of the twentieth century. My grandparents grew up during the 1920s through the 1940s, when there was no TV. Instead, they listened to the radio for news, entertainment, and to stay connected. The right to vote for my grandmother was still a relatively new development, established with the passage of the Nineteenth Amendment in 1920. Unions were becoming more common and stronger, allowing White workers to support their families and escape poverty, thereby cultivating a middle class. All my grandparents remembered reading

---

31. Lola Méndez, "A Brief Explainer on Latine and Latinx," *Hispanic Executive,* June 5, 2023, https://hispanicexecutive.com/latinx-latine-explainer/.

about and hearing radio news reports on the NAACP lawsuits for voting rights, anti-lynching legislation, and employment antidiscrimination laws. The start of World War II sparked military enlistment among my grandfathers, and my grandmothers joined the Rosie the Riveter movement alongside other women, in every area of the workforce.[32]

My parents' generation grew up during the 1950s through the 1960s. They grew up with some TV, watching shows such as the *Ed Sullivan Show, Ozzie & Harriet*, and *Leave It To Beaver*. Those last two were part of a societal messaging campaign following WWII to show that women were eager to return to their traditional roles as wives and mothers. Both of my parents remembered the passage of the Civil Rights Act in 1964 and recalled the horror of watching White police officers beating nonviolent Black protesters as young teenagers. Later, in the 1960s, my father started college and tried to join the army (medically denied) to fight in the war in Vietnam. At the same time, my mother worked at an art store and protested the war. She also fought for equal rights for women, including reproductive freedom.

All three of our generations lived through and experienced the modernization of technology and society. My grandparents got landline phones in their homes as teenagers, and

---

32. See appendix C to learn about some BIPOC women I wish I'd learned about sooner.

my parents grew up with TV, phones, refrigerators, and a coal furnace. My parents' home included the technology they grew up with, along with a dishwasher, washer and dryer, and baseboard heating. Phones became cordless, call waiting became a call function, and answering machines became commonplace. In the 1980s and '90s, we were no longer dependent on radio, 8-tracks, or record players to listen to music. Boomboxes, Walkmans, and CD players became the latest gadgets every young person needed. Yet even as society and technology progressed, racism was always there.

Across all three generations, civil rights and **racial justice** were national issues of conversation. My grandparents didn't see themselves as a part of the national conversation because they didn't know a lot of Black and Brown people. They assumed they were good because they weren't as racist as those in the Jim Crow areas of the country, and they figured it was a Black and Brown problem to address. My parents didn't see themselves as a part of the national conversations because they were more focused on the Vietnam War and the Equal Rights Amendment, which affected them much more directly.

All my pillars of socialization helped me develop a sense of empathy. The lessons of fairness, justice, and freedom weren't nuanced in any way, but they did instill those values in me. Witnessing the pain of families, colleagues, and the nation following the *Challenger* explosion and the Chernobyl disaster left an imprint on my soul, and watching the video of Rodney King being brutally beaten by LAPD officers in 1991 was a horrifying reminder that racism was not a thing of the past. But it still felt external to me.

I will never forget the horror I felt throughout my entire being when I learned of the beating and rape of Abner Louima by NYPD officers in 1997. Mr. Louima was wrongfully arrested, beaten by multiple officers multiple times while in custody, and sodomized by an officer while handcuffed. As details emerged of the barbaric assault and Mr. Louima's injuries, I threw up. My heart broke for this man. The incident increased my awareness and understanding that racism was everywhere in our society, yet I still saw it as just something outside of me.

During the first half of my life, I had great empathy for those struggling with mental health, people who were cash poor and experiencing houselessness, and people living with HIV or AIDS. I realize now that this was due to my proximity to people who were experiencing these things and the societal biases and stigmas surrounding them. I had a clearer understanding of the disconnect between the stories told about these people and the reality of who they were as human beings. I saw the fear they carried, the pain and the masking they did to hide it, their fear of being disposable. And I saw the invisibility they felt as they were ignored and othered. I had less empathy for identities I had less proximity to, while absorbing narratives about them through the media. I absorbed messages about people, even those I didn't have relationships with or know—that they were inherently dangerous, not to be trusted, and in some way *less than*.

It was easy for me to resist the idea of my racism. I was told throughout my life that I was not racist, and though I learned to look down on the times of slavery and Jim Crow, I accepted that there was a significant distance between me and where overtly racist acts took place. It was easy for me to resist my racism without having the context of historical racism or the present-day manifestations of it. It was easy to resist my racism without having meaningful relationships with Black and Brown people. And it was easy to ignore my racism by seeing people only for what I'd been told about them.

Maintaining my resistance allowed me to stay connected with my perception of my goodness. For too long, like my familial generations that came before me, I did not see myself as a part of the national and local conversations on civil rights and racial justice. I assumed my goodness because I wasn't a racist in the ways my grandparents' and parents' generations were, nor was I overtly racist like the KKK or some other White supremacist group. I followed the rules and was obedient.

After months of leading anti-profiling trainings for SPD officers and still feeling uncertain in the antiracism work I was doing, Cherese—my respected, seasoned racial justice mentor from the Office for Civil Rights—invited me to coffee. At the coffee shop, Cherese was finishing a meeting with a striking, affectionate woman named Esme, a veteran traffic enforcement officer and fellow SPD anti-profiling facilitator, who enamored me. When introduced, Esme surprised me with an uncharacteristically long and grounding hug, saying, "Honey, you're in the community now. We have to love each other while we're operating in a world that can't offer us that." This small act of deep care, though overwhelming, planted a seed of belonging in a world I was still unsure how to navigate.

We all sat at the table. After debriefing the SPD trainings, Cherese posed a pivotal question to us: "How do you two feel about helping reestablish the SPD Change Team and being its coleads?" The panic I felt when the police headquarters first called me to facilitate the anti-profiling trainings resurfaced. I was already feeling overextended, exhausted, and self-doubting, and my mind began to race: *Damn it, Cherese! This is happening so fast. Once again, I'll be exposed as not good enough.* But Cherese gave me her knowing look—a look that said, "Don't choose comfort over commitment"—and it nudged me toward risk.

After Cherese spoke to us about our new racial justice work, Esme asked, "Are we doing this?"

"I'm in if you're in," I replied cautiously but sincerely. And so began our imperfect, shared leadership journey.

Then came the defining moment of mutual account-ability. Cherese's final words before departing affirmed the cross-racial solidarity we were building: "Casey, your job is to have Esme's back. Use your privilege to lift her voice up and interrupt harms directed at her, okay?"

Esme chimed in, "I'm counting on you."

"I'll do my best," I offered.

"Or better than your best," Esme laughed. "Help me get to my twenty years so I can retire."

I understood my assignment and said, "I will learn to do my new best."

After a year of struggle and limited results, we were both invited to join the prestigious Race and Social Justice Initiative (RSJI) "CORE" Team. Some folks said that CORE stood for "City Organizers for Racial Equity," while others said it meant we would become part of the core networks for the RSJI Strategy Team. Either way, I felt humbled and honored by the invitation but doubtful about leaning in further. However, by this point I'd learned that if something felt scary in this way, it was likely exposing one of my growing edges.

Beginning my personal antiracism journey was accidental, and it wasn't pretty.

Chapter 9

MY FRAGILITY EXPOSED

How My Fear of Being Seen as Racist Kept Me from Doing the Work

I attended my first facilitated race-based **caucus** in 2008 as I began working more closely with the RSJI. A race-based caucus is an opportunity for Black people, People of Color, multiracial people, White people, and people of other racial identities to come together in race-based groups and engage in discussions about their racial identities. These race-based spaces offer the opportunity for people to discuss their experiences of navigating society in relation to their racial identity among others who share that identity, and they allow people to discuss current challenges and events openly. For many, these spaces provide a space for healing and solace and to unlearn societal narratives and messages about race, racism, and racial identities. These spaces also offer an opportunity to learn and gain greater self-awareness in racial identities, particularly for White people, who must think about their racial identity the least.

My first White caucus took place in Seattle City Hall's Bertha Knight Landes Room, one of the most beautiful city spaces in Seattle. It can comfortably accommodate a few hundred people, and two sides of the large room feature floor-to-ceiling windows overlooking downtown and Elliott Bay. It's always in pristine condition. I was terrified to attend. I didn't know what to expect and was perpetually afraid of being exposed as ignorant or not a good person. I wasn't sure how I was supposed to show up, what was expected of me, or how I should engage. I'd been raised to always be fifteen minutes early to any event, but that felt risky. I didn't want to be too early and have to speak to anyone before we started, so for thirteen minutes I hid in one of the bathroom stalls and anxiously checked the time every ten to fifteen seconds.

As the caucus start time neared, I felt my breath getting shorter. When I left the bathroom and walked into the event, I saw a few older White women huddled together to the side. They appeared to know each other well, as evident by their warm and affectionate engagement with one another. I could feel my nerve endings vibrating, and my hypervigilant tendencies were on high alert. I scanned the room to see who was there, observing how people engaged or didn't engage with others, and I identified the exit routes in the room in case I needed a quick escape.

I could see that there were around thirty to forty chairs set up in a circle in the middle of the room, which looked more like doll furniture in such a large space. There were two female facilitators, one Black and one White, standing by two central chairs, talking to each other in soft voices, and scanning the room with an intensity I'd seen only in classrooms. As my conditioning had taught me, good students sit close to the teacher when possible, so I slowly put my backpack on a chair near the facilitators. The White facilitator encouraged me to take a seat, stating we'd start soon. I smiled and did as I was told. As the facilitators wrangled the other participants to the circle, I prayed no one would sit in the other chairs next to me. An occupied chair next to me would make it more difficult to leave. Only about half of the chairs were filled, which was strange because the **BIPOC** caucus seemed to have a larger number of attendees and was meeting in a small conference room upstairs.

The White facilitator called the caucus together and, before introductions, led us through a land acknowledgment and breathing exercise. I'd never heard of a land acknowledgment before and was surprised to learn it centered on the Indigenous people and land of the city called Seattle. The closest thing I'd ever heard to an acknowledgment of land was "God's green Earth." In my primary school, we learned only a tiny bit about the Indigenous people of Suffolk County, Long Island, such as the Montauk, Shinnecock, Corchaug, and Secatogue, and so many more. The caucus was also the first time I'd heard the term "occupied land" when referring to the land on which we existed, Duwamish land. At that moment, I felt incredibly ignorant and ashamed, as my title was "Inclusive Outreach and Engagement Specialist" and I'd honestly never considered the land anything but American soil—a reality that embarrassed me. To reassure myself, I remembered that this was my first caucus and I was learning. I told myself that I could stay quiet during the conversation, which increased my comfort.

As the breathing exercise began, all I could think was, *What the fuck is this?* My hypervigilance would not allow me to close my eyes, feel my feet root into the ground, or take deep breaths. Relaxing equated to a feeling of vulnerability and a sense of being out of control, and that was not a practice I was comfortable with, so I supportively watched other participants do it.

The introductions then started, during which the facilitators invited us to share our names, our roles at the city, the departments we worked in, and our racial identities. Once again, my nerve endings were electrified. I'd never sat in a room with other White people and named our racial identities. Hearing other people identify themselves as White felt good; I'd never engaged in conversation like this before and it was refreshing. The adults in my family talked about race with hateful and demeaning language, usually directed at Black and Brown people, and other adults in my life spoke about race and racism in whispers, usually in the direction of Black and Brown people. This was my first experience talking about being White, having a White racial identity in the US, and Whiteness.

After introductions, the facilitators asked us to reflect on and identify ways racism had manifested in our work and lives over the last week. I felt another wave of panic and intimidation wash over me. As the wave began to wane, I noticed my remaining feelings of dread. I had no idea how to answer the question. My feeling of inadequacy rose right back up to the surface in my body. I'd partly committed to this being a learning and absorbing moment for me so that I could stay silent in the space, and this question meant I might have to share. The rapid-fire thoughts stemming from my fear and anxiety filled the period of time for reflection. I hadn't thought of anything.

Thankfully, another participant shared examples of ways she had observed racism around her to get us started. The facilitators thanked her for getting the conversation going and asked follow-up questions, such as, "Would you say that was **individual racism**, **interpersonal racism**, **institutional racism**, **systemic racism**, or **cultural racism**?" I didn't hear the participant's answers because all I was thinking was, *Holy shit that's a lot of racism, and I'm so glad I don't have to speak up.*

The White facilitator asked what the participant did when she witnessed examples of racism. She remained quiet for a few moments, no more than a minute, but it felt like an hour. The facilitators even stopped other participants from jumping in: "Let her speak; you'll have a chance to share." It was incredible how quickly we had transitioned from a grounding and a breathing exercise to a quiet, robust tension. Almost everyone was immobilized.

Finally, the speaking participant offered, "I saw it."

The Black facilitator chimed in, speaking in a soothing tone, "And that is important, but then what did you do? Did you say something to the aggressor? Did you seek help? Did you check in on the person on the receiving end of that encounter?"[33]

As the participant responded, her terse words tightened and her volume increased. "No, but I'm not the bad one here."

The White facilitator responded, "No one said that."

The Black facilitator followed up with, "The aggressor was the initiator of harm. Let me ask you, how do you think inaction can cause harm?"

Most of us White participants sat quietly and stared at the floor. I could only imagine others felt as uncomfortable and as relieved as I did that we weren't the ones in the hot seat.

The participant began crying and stated she didn't feel safe in this space, then grabbed her things and headed for the door. Before leaving, she turned to the group to say, "I am a good person, and I am not a racist."

---

33. See appendix D for The Five D's of Bystander Intervention.

I felt bad for the facilitators because we had barely begun the caucus. I felt bad for the Black facilitator because her gentle questioning was both uncomfortable and supportive, like a tutor guiding us through a difficult study session. I also felt bad for the participant. While I didn't know all the feelings she was experiencing, she left early, something I'd given myself permission to do before the caucus even started. I felt very uncomfortable but not unsafe. Physically, I'd experienced various forms of violence in the first twenty-plus years of my life, but in that caucus moment I felt physically safe. The discomfort I was experiencing was rooted in my self-perception and my desire to be seen as a nonracist, good person by others.

When I went home that night, I imagined myself in each of the facilitators' positions, as well as in the position of the participant who spoke up. I also explored my feelings about my nonparticipatory engagement. As a White facilitator, I might have felt frustrated at how easy it was to avoid the intended and needed conversation and sad that my cofacilitator had to experience that moment. I might have felt disappointed in my fellow White folks for disengaging so quickly, and I might have dreaded reporting back to the other groups and caucus facilitators.

I can never know what it feels like to be Black or Brown in America.

As I reflected on the exchange between the facilitator and the participant, I remembered the facilitator's face.

She had beautiful natural hair wrapped in a colorful scarf positioned atop her head, and she wore large, circular black glasses with thick rims. Her face was round, and her smile was beautiful, the corners of her mouth extending high up to her cheekbones. When I reflected on how she looked, I also saw someone committed to having the needed conversation and her unwavering commitment to racial justice work. I had seen the subtle, deep breaths she was taking as silence filled the room, and I'd seen her lean into the circle as most of us, being White, were silent, staring at the floor, and leaning away. I also saw her eyelids blink and her mouth tighten as she seemed both unsurprised and disappointed that the participant had walked out of the room.

As a fellow participant, I imagined the shame spiral I would've gone down. I thought about how sad I might have felt about myself and how afraid I might have felt about what others thought of me. I imagined the embarrassment and fearing the word getting out to my coworkers and managers about how racist I was. As a fellow White participant, I wanted to distance myself from the White participant who'd walked out of the room. Even though I'd considered doing the exact same thing, some of my initial thoughts after the caucus included, *Well, I wouldn't have done that; I'm nothing like my racist family members, so no one thinks I'm racist; I'm from New York, so I'm not racist; I don't say (overtly) racist things, so I'm good*; and a myriad of other thoughts that allowed me to villainize the other participant and excuse myself from examining my racism. Initially, these thoughts also allowed me to reassure myself of my goodness.

Once I was home, I wondered whether I would've been brave enough to speak up, whether I would've been able to answer any of the facilitators' questions, and how I would've reacted differently if I'd taken a risk to speak up and was nudged to dig deeper. I didn't like what was coming up for me. I wanted to be the kind of person who was willing to speak up and take risks and who could receive constructive feedback or criticism well. I did want to be that person, but I was the person who hid in the bathroom. I was the person with the exit strategy. I was the person who permitted myself to be silent.

At this point in my personal antiracism work, I had heard dozens, if not hundreds, of Black and Brown people share their stories and experiences of racism. I began to think about how it must have felt to share a personal story or experience or an aspect of lived reality only to be ignored, dismissed, or disputed. The White caucus space was designed for reflection and introspection; we were aware of this going into the space. So why was it so hard for us to do it? For me, attending the caucus had initially been about visibility. I'd wanted my boss and manager to see I was actively participating in the RSJI program, as they'd given me permission to do so; I wanted the RSJI team to know I was attending the events they'd invited me to; and I wanted the other people involved in RSJI to see I was attending these intentional conversations. But being seen and being present isn't the same as engagement. Engaging in the caucus space required deep reflection and sometimes painful truths, such as how I'd been raised not to believe or trust Black and Brown people. Ultimately, it was in caucus spaces and in relationships I built with the people I met in them where I received the support needed to unpack my own racism.

My conscious mind desperately wanted to excavate my racism, and my body wanted to resist feeling this painful discomfort. I'd learned to numb and sterilize the connection between my mind and my body and that being a good person meant following the rules. My family set the rules, and my family told me we were good people and not racists. My school set the rules, and my school taught me that slavery was bad, that Jim Crow laws were bad, and that we were a better and fairer country now. My church set the rules, and my church taught me that if I followed God and God's rules, I was a good person and would go to heaven. The media set the rules, showing White people as cops, firefighters, government leaders, and the good guys. Collectively, all these rules taught me that any societal inequities were due to personal character flaws. I still wanted to be good, I wanted to be better, but I felt uncertain about how to proceed as I was challenging everything I'd learned and believed.

I wanted to permit myself to lean into that automatic response of shutting down or closing myself off to what felt uncomfortable. But I pictured the Black facilitator's face and knew I owed her and every other Black and Brown person who shared their truths with me the dignity of pushing through my insecurity, shame, and guilt. I owed each of those people the respect of examining my insecurities and the decency of my humility, my **cultural humility**.[34] My biggest challenge was that I didn't know how to do it or where to start. My anxiety and discomfort often tried convincing me that I'd done enough or had arrived at an antiracism way of being so that I could again convince myself that I was good, that I was not racist anymore. One way I attempted to support this narrative was by seeking formal and informal assurances from Black and Brown individuals. I'd approach RSJI staff, volunteers, and external contractors, aiming to align myself with them by offering to help set up, talking about my antiracism work in SPD, or acting as if I understood when others in the space didn't. I used the latest terminology and asked for their thoughts on new research or

---

34. Cultural humility is "an approach to understanding and respecting the cultural identities of individuals and communities … [C]ultural humility focuses on a lifelong commitment to self-evaluation and self-critique": "Cultural Humility—Definition and Explanation," *The Oxford Review*, accessed May 28, 2024, https://oxford-review. com/the-oxford-review-dei-diversity-equity-and-inclusion-dictionary/ cultural-humility-definition-and-explanation/.

recent news developments. I was driven by an unconscious need to be perceived as good by Black and Brown people, yet I still wasn't listening. I was still centering myself, what *I* needed, and my comfort in those interactions under the guise of being helpful or on board with dismantling racism.

The most potent truth and awareness I gained at this time was that it is not enough to see racism only in others, institutions, and systems. We, myself included, must excavate it from ourselves. We need to address it in our circles of influence and existing pillars of socialization. As for me, I needed to sit in the discomfort of my resistance to antiracism. I needed to consistently ask myself, *Am I racist?* and to sit in the discomfort of that question and its answer. I needed to explore and examine all aspects of myself, including how I thought, what I believed, how I listened, how I behaved in various situations, how I was curious, where I was causing unintended harm, where I needed to soften, and where I needed to grow.

Reflection is one of the most important and frequently ignored actions we White folks can take when we choose to lean into antiracism work. This action requires us to move past our learned understanding of goodness, being good, and being good enough, and it supports us in moving beyond our shame, fear, and guilt.

While I was participating in antiracism work and beginning my caucus work, I was also dealing with a deeply personal and painful situation. I had to set a hard boundary with my mother, who'd been harassing me for years by writing letters, calling my workplaces to discredit me, taking out loans in my name, and even having people physically assault me. I hadn't responded to her toxic behaviors in nearly a decade, but things escalated when she emailed my supervisor, my director, the mayor's office, and the city council to have me fired and exposed as a fraud. During a check-in conversation with Ellis, I braced myself for termination. Instead, she responded with compassion, asking if I was okay and offering support. She connected me with someone in the police department's victim assistance unit, which was a turning point for me. Despite keeping my work and personal life separate, I now had to face this intersection, but I was supported in doing so.

While I was learning about systemic racism, I realized I was benefiting from the very systems I was critiquing; I had access to legal support, language fluency, and financial means. Still, navigating family court to get a restraining order against my mother was terrifying and one of the hardest things I've ever done. I thought I understood the system, but the reality was overwhelming—especially when I saw women across racial lines with visible injuries denied protection.

In the end, I got the restraining order. The judge was so disturbed by a letter my mother had mailed directly to the court that he wouldn't read it aloud or let me see it. That moment underscored not only how traumatic the experience was but also how much **White privilege** I had in being able to access protection. Going through this while doing antiracism work gave me a deeper understanding of trauma, oppression, and the complexity of such privilege. I'd experienced long-term childhood abuse and carried multiple minoritized identities, so I knew trauma, bias, and discrimination affected me negatively. But this was one of my first moments acknowledging the benefits I experienced as a White person. Taking my abusive mother to court allowed me to have a boundary with my terrorizer. The court heard me. The court believed and trusted me. The judge said, "The letter your mother wrote gives me a good idea of what you've been dealing with here. I'm sorry. No one should ever have to read a letter like this, especially from their parent." I burst into tears and my whole body shook. The validation that came from an authority figure saying that what I was experiencing wasn't right, noting that I deserved better, and supporting me in setting that boundary changed me. I felt a glimmer of empowerment.

After the validation of my protection order, I worked with my therapist, mentors, and friends to identify what permission slips I needed to write for myself to help untangle my racism and its roots. By writing these permission slips, I was able to hold onto my conscious values and be open to new ways of existing that centered on collective humanity, not just myself.

Permission Slips

ENCOURAGEMENT NOTES TO MOVE BEYOND SHAME, GUILT, AND FEAR

- I give myself permission to take my time processing this new awareness.
- I give myself permission to be new and open to learning information outside of my original pillars.
- I give myself permission to be accountable and be held accountable without judgment of myself or the person holding me accountable.
- I give myself permission to feel my feelings and process them in new ways without judgment or timelines.
- I give myself permission to make mistakes as I begin to learn without self-judgment.
- I give myself permission to let go of obligations that require my needs to be minimized and to recognize the many options available in my days, relationships, mindsets, and beliefs.
- I give myself permission to not always do what others expect of me or think I should do, without judgment.
- I give myself permission to believe I am worthy of love, respect, care, and kindness because I am a human being.
- I give myself permission to let go of what I've always known, done, or believed.
- I give myself permission to feel and sit in discomfort.
- I give myself permission to believe and trust new sources of information.
- I give myself permission to trust myself and not seek approval or external affirmation from anyone who requires subjugation from me, at all times and in every area of my existence.

Figure 4

Chapter 10

I THOUGHT I WAS FURTHER ALONG

Confronting the Distance Between My Intentions and My Impact

My initial resistance to the idea that racism, **sexism**, and bias aren't just external but also internal was deeply rooted in my insecurities. I had spent my life striving to be good, to be seen as good, to be good enough. The possibility that bias and **prejudice** could live inside me challenged not only my self-image but the foundation of my moral identity. It felt unbearable, even unforgivable.

Esme and I were accepted into the RSJI CORE Team program. I was humbled but felt doubtful about being included in such a powerful group of cross-racial people in various positions who were leading the work across the city. These were people I admired, and this was when I would remind myself that if something felt scary, that was a growing edge in my antiracism analysis development.

The CORE Team was a three-year commitment. In preparation for the start of the program, I took two online Implicit Association Tests through Project Implicit, one on race and one on gender. Project Implicit is a nonprofit organization founded by three academic researchers: Dr. Mahzarin Banaji (Harvard University), Dr. Brian Nosek (University of Virginia), and Dr. Tony Greenwald (University of Washington). The organization aims to illuminate and educate the public about their unconscious or **implicit biases**, which are shaped by social conditioning from the primary pillars of our socialization and often lead to **internalized racism**. The tests are simple and fast, rapidly presenting images and words for the test taker to sort into good and bad or right and wrong. Once the test is completed, the results reveal whether the taker has a "strong preference" for one identity or another, has a "slight preference" for one identity or another, or is "neutral" to both identities. I assumed I'd be "neutral" when it came to racial identities with all my RSJI work over the last few years, with a "slight preference" for females when it came to gender. (The tests on gender use the binary categories of "male" and "female.") And because I was socialized as female, I assumed I'd have a preference for women.

To my horror, I was wrong according to both of my test results. I showed a strong preference for White people and a strong preference for males. I felt shocked, defeated, and annoyed. The shock stemmed from my internal perception that I should've been further along in my personal work than the test results indicated. The defeat came from wondering how I would ever overcome my preference for White people if I still had a preference for men while being raised as a female. The annoyance was at my pillars of socialization for deeply ingraining me with racist and sexist messages, as well as for unconsciously preferring White people and men when my conscious self did not. This moment illuminated how much more personal work I needed to do to address the racism and sexism that existed within me. It served as a reminder to accept that my personal work to unpack my racism would be lifelong and ever-evolving, because there is no definitive endpoint. And it helped me recognize that my resistance came from interpreting an unwelcome reality as a judgment of my character rather than as useful information for my personal antiracism development.

My heart rate increased as I reviewed my results. I consciously didn't want racism within me, but my conscious mind, unconscious mind, heart, and body weren't aligned. Berating thoughts of shame activated inside me. *This can't be*, I thought. *I have Black friends*, I thought. *I'm nice to everyone*, I thought. I couldn't bear the fact that so much of what I'd been taught or learned from people I loved and trusted was rooted in racism and insufficient. I was embarrassed to have been so trusting of the messaging

I'd received and absorbed to the point where I never doubted or questioned it.

Leaning into developing an antiracist analysis and engaging in antiracism work required me to acknowledge several additional truths. Despite being a rising star in the field of emergency management, when it came to antiracism work I was in my infancy; after seventeen years of academic education, I had a lot more to learn. I'd been taught to compete with and measure myself against others as benchmarks of my worth, but in antiracism work I was joining a movement of collective work. No one was looking at me to fix everything. I was welcomed, seen, accepted, and included in antiracism spaces as myself while also not being centered.

As the distance between my family and me continued to increase as a result of my setting boundaries with my mother and coming out, I craved an intimate connection and a sense of belonging. However, as I entered this new space, I realized I needed to listen more and speak less. While no one expected perfection from me, I needed to work through my discomfort while making mistakes, especially mistakes that put my perceived goodness at risk in the eyes of others.

One shift I had to make to support leaning into antiracism was moving toward internal validation practices rather than constantly seeking external validation. I also needed to define what "good" and "goodness" meant to me. Instead of worrying about speaking up and getting in trouble or upsetting authority figures, such as bosses, if I noticed or felt something wasn't right, I owed it to myself and others to speak up. That felt good.

Another shift I needed to make was how I listened to others, especially people with identities different from my own. I was raised to listen to and follow instructions and to respond with solutions to what was said. Instead, I needed to listen to the other person's words and the emotions behind them and then shift to responding with open curiosity and care. That felt not only good but more authentic.

I was raised to be nice, which meant smiling, saying "please" and "thank you," and being well-mannered so as not to create a disturbance or make others uncomfortable. What I needed was to shift to being kind. Kindness demonstrates care for a fellow human being and an investment in their well-being. Being kind felt good. I also needed to shift from thinking only about myself, my family, and those I cared about to thinking about our collective societal well-being, health, and safety. That, too, felt good.

An enormous and difficult shift I needed to make was offering myself forgiveness and releasing my shame, fear, and guilt for not having seen racism in the world and in myself before stumbling into this work. Forgiveness toward myself and others felt good because it created space for compassion, empathy, humility, vulnerability, and growth, which also felt honest and real.

It was a privilege to have the gift of a three-year antiracism program to support my unlearning, learning, and personal transformation. The first year was dedicated to relationship-building, unlearning, and learning. We built relationships with all members in our cohort as well as with those in the second year of the program, our mentors. I had essential relationships in my life before this opportunity, yet nothing prepared me for the powerful, authentic, and intimate relationships I cultivated with many of the people in the program, including with one of the most brilliant people I've ever met, Champagne. Champagne has the biggest heart. She's anchored in love, and it radiates from her. We were both twenty-seven years old when we met, and our energies amplified each other. The first time we met for a relationship-building meeting, we scheduled forty-five minutes but ended up meeting for three hours. When we finally began to say goodbye, we asked each other for a hug, held each other, and didn't let go for at least three minutes.

The depth of relationships I was able to build through the program with people like Esme and Champagne changed how I built relationships throughout my life. Open, honest, raw, authentic, and accountable dialogue became a new requirement in my relationships, as did prioritizing people over tasks and linear time. Leaning into relationships rooted in love, care, kindness, and empathy allowed me to shed my societal masks and uncover more of my true self. The ability to call bullshit and be called out on my bullshit supported trust-building in my relationships and got easier with experience and time.

The second year served more as an internship during which we supported our mentors in a **racial equity** project of their choosing, assisted with RSJI work in our respective departments, and built on our first year of learning. Each of us also began mentoring those in their first year of the program. The third year included everything from the second year, except that Esme and I were tasked with supporting SPD in creating an RSJI work plan for the following year.

Working in collaboration with Esme, the CORE Team, and the team from RSJI allowed me to learn and develop a deeper racial analysis with immense support. This network was intergenerational, cross-racial, and inclusive of various genders and a multitude of diverse identities. We were all expected to learn from each other, and when conflict arose, we were meant to work through it without external intervention. We were also expected to recognize where our identities had privileges, identify where and how we experienced oppression, and speak about both with ease and clarity. We had an abundance of support while understanding that these practices and expectations would feel uncomfortable.

I needed support to practice antiracism. I still do. I needed to develop the ability to be comfortable with discomfort, to develop the ability to sit without certainty, closure, or resolution. I needed to listen, trust, and believe the voices of Black and Brown individuals when they shared their lived experiences, and I also needed to speak up and use my voice and not just expect Black and Brown people to do the work. I had a role in supporting antiracism everywhere, and I needed to acknowledge that, as well as recognize that antiracism efforts, terminology, practices, and leaders would evolve over time. In essence, to maintain my commitment to antiracism and justice, I would need to continue evolving and adapting.

Now, when I work with organizations starting, engaging in, or struggling with diversity, equity, inclusion, belonging, and accessibility (DEIBA) initiatives and efforts, I try to remember that no matter where people of the organization are in this work, I've been there too. I've been the person who resists a reality they don't want to believe, the person who was silent because they were uncomfortable and didn't want to say the wrong thing or cause harm, the person who struggled with what they were learning. I've been outraged at my fellow White people for not believing or for dismissing Black and Brown voices to demonstrate my goodness, and I've been the person whose voice cracks and eyes well with tears at the enormity of harm. I've also been the person who defers to the reaction of those in the room with the most institutional power. As a facilitator, my role is to hold space, read a group's energy, and adjust as needed, creating an environment that fosters vulnerability, authenticity, and accountability while centering the experiences and impacts of Black and Brown participants.

Many years after completing the program, I was supporting a mid-sized, well-funded start-up company. The leaders were "very committed" to equity, took pride in their DEI initiatives and podcast, and even discussed packaging their equity work and selling it to other companies. Unfortunately, there was a substantial disconnect between the leadership's perspective on their DEI work and the experiences of Black and Brown employees at the company—not uncommon within organizations. Another contractor, a Black woman named Pat, had invited me into the work. One of the first things she said to me was, "I think they want to be equitable and committed. The challenge is, they don't listen to anything they don't want to hear, they ignore Black and Brown people, and if anyone tries to talk with leadership, leadership tells them how ungrateful they are and how great the company is doing in their equity work." Pat had been working with them for years and was exhausted.

Pat and I collaborated to design a workshop series for the company's leadership, which included a timeline review of their DEI work and established a baseline understanding of antiracism work at the organizational, individual leader, and collective leadership levels. We analyzed personal behaviors, organizational culture, and organizational practices to identify and mitigate bias in these areas. Additionally, we identified antiracism goals and work plans. However, because the leaders wouldn't acknowledge their limited progress in their antiracism work, their employees perceived their DEI efforts as a joke and performative. For example, the company hosted internal annual awards to recognize employees for outstanding work; beginning in 2021, the leadership team created an award category for DEI efforts and awarded it to themselves annually. One of the main barriers to meaningful DEI work was the founder and CEO, Mortimer, and the rest of the leadership team's acquiescence to him.

Mortimer was a straight, White male born in the early 1950s. He was nice, spoke with all employees regardless of position, and hosted lunch hours for all staff. But he was so stuck in his idea of himself as a good leader that he refused to explore being an equitable leader. He said in one workshop, "I can't be racist; I grew up in the seventies." When I asked him to explain, he crossed his arms and told me I wouldn't understand. I asked him to try me, and instead of responding he pulled out his phone and played Helen Reddy's "I Am Woman (Hear Me Roar)." The other leaders remained silent, staring at the desk. It was an awkward moment that illuminated why their DEI initiatives were continuing to fail and remained in the performative realm: leadership was incapable of acknowledging their own lack of progress, and other leaders deferred to the behavior of the person with the most power.

Prior to our final workshop, I assigned questions for leadership to reflect on and discuss in the last session:

- What biases do you have that you're working to address?
- Who first taught you about race and racism? What did you learn?
- When was the last time you perpetuated a **microaggression** due to work overload? When did you realize it? How did you address it?
- What strategies and tools do you use to interrupt bias and/or microaggressions?

There were eight people on the leadership team. I assigned each question to two of the leaders so we could have a more robust and concentrated discussion, and I assigned Mortimer the question about microaggressions. I did this because I'd heard about some of the profoundly problematic microaggressions he committed regularly, including assuming every Latine employee spoke Spanish and mandating that they sing "Feliz Navidad" with him at the holiday party, approaching **transgender** employees and asking them to speak to all staff about why transgender people want to be included in sports, and asking Black employees where they felt their responsibility lay in resolving conflicts with leadership regarding DEI initiatives.

The other person I assigned to that question was Farren, another senior leader, and he offered an honest and vulnerable example to start the conversation. Though Farren had once been as problematic as Mortimer, he had begun to make shifts to become a better and more equitable leader.

Then it was Mortimer's turn to share. "I don't have an example. I've never done a microaggression," he stated.

"Mortimer, never?" I asked.

"No," he persisted.

"I shared a list of examples of common microaggressions with you, yes? You've never committed any of them?" I asked, referring to a handout I used to highlight everyday microaggressions that typically occur in a workplace.

"What if I asked you, 'When was the last time you beat your wife?' That's basically what you're asking me," he retorted.

Mortimer's response left me speechless. It's challenging when participants present this level of resistance because, as a human, I want to respond personally, but I also have a responsibility to the others in the room. I had to address the response, both because I didn't know what any participant's home life was like or whether they had a domestic violence history and because this behavior was a distraction from the conversation.

He kept going, his voice elevating and his finger pointing in my face. "Really, when was the last time you beat your wife?" Then he pointed at the only Person of Color in the room and said, "Or you?"

"Mortimer, I'm going to have to ask you to stop right now. Domestic violence and microaggressions are not the same. I find this analogy offensive," I said in a low voice to help deescalate the conversation.

His face became bright red as the blood rushed up his neck. He stood up, kicked his chair back with his right foot, and stormed out of the emergency door.

I called a fifteen-minute break, and several of the other leaders, all men, chased after him to comfort him. The two female leaders stayed behind in the room. One looked at me and mouthed "thank you," and the other grabbed my hand to hold and with tears in her eyes shared, "This happens all the time."

As I walked out of the building through the main entrance, Farren stopped me. "I used to want to be him," he said, "but not anymore. I've been a problem in the past, not taking DEI seriously, and I want to be a part of the solution. Thank you for being here with us."

I still needed to take a few moments to regroup from Mortimer's outburst, but my exchange with Farren reminded me that people exist on a spectrum of racism and antiracism. I thanked him for sharing with me and invited him to speak up when he disagreed with Mortimer or his behavior during the remainder of our time together. He took a deep breath and nodded. I watched him fidget in his chair and stare down at the table as the workshop reconvened. I knew he was uncomfortable, and I knew he was nervous because we both knew it wouldn't be long before Mortimer provided an opportunity for Farren to demonstrate a new approach to his DEI work.

For the first hour after the break, Mortimer sat in a chair at a table by himself with his arms crossed. His lips were cinched tightly, and he occasionally audibly exhaled as others participated in the workshop. When he finally stood up and began walking over to the table where the other leaders were sitting, he raised his hand in the air and began to speak: "Can I just say something about all this inclusion of sensitive people?" His tone was as irksome as his question. I braced myself for what was coming, preparing for another horrifying exchange.

"No, Mortimer!" Farren cried out.

The room got quiet. You could feel the tense energy at the leaders' table. I tried not to smile.

Farren continued with a quiet and firm tone. "You are being disruptive. I, like you, have received negative feedback from our employees, but unlike you, I am interested in improving. That won't happen if you continue to take up all the oxygen in the room."

Farren's risk at that moment shifted the dynamics of the leadership team. He showed the other leaders that they had a lot more work to do on their individual and collective journeys and that not everything they credited themselves for was reality. Farren exposed how closed the leadership team was to real DEI work and that some leaders were willing to learn, while others dismissed anything they didn't want to believe or were most comfortable with the company's status quo. If I had focused only on Mortimer's resistance, ego, and desire to be seen as good, I wouldn't have been able to expose his **White fragility** and problematic behavior. I also wouldn't have been able to support Farren in his development.

There are open and overt racists in society. Some people think antiracism isn't their issue because they're not a Black or Brown person, some are taught and want to believe in **colorblindness**, and some legitimately don't know about the present-day manifestations of racism. There are people who are open to learning, changing their behaviors, and causing less harm, and some actively want to dismantle systemic and societal racism. You never genuinely know where people stand in their personal antiracism journeys until these conversations begin.

The consequences of not acknowledging where we are in our racial analysis or antiracism journey are substantial. To start with, it tells Black and Brown people we're comfortable with the harms of their oppression. For another, it limits our ability to connect with and build relationships with people of various racial identities while supporting the maintenance of systems that cause harm to Black and Brown communities. It also denies the humanity of Black and Brown people and limits our ability to see our own humanity.

Chapter 11

FROM WANTING TO BE GOOD TO CHOOSING TO DO GOOD

How Self-Reflection Rewired My Commitment to Antiracism

Once I consciously redefined what "good," "goodness," and "good enough" meant for me, I had to work to absorb this new reality. My muscle memory fought my new conscious definitions. For many years, I chose to walk several miles to work to support transforming my muscle memory and use the time to reflect. I thought about my new definitions, my new awarenesses, my frustrations with all I didn't know, my curiosities around what was possible, and a myriad of other ruminations.

Reflection is one of the most important antiracist actions we can take. Reflection takes time, and carving out that time takes intention. I worked in emergency management and engaged in inclusive community outreach, which meant attending government meetings between 7:00 a.m. and 5:00 p.m. and community meetings and gatherings between 6:00 p.m. and 9:00 p.m. Emergencies happened at any time. I was also trying to have a social life. There was hardly time for rest, let alone for pause and process. Being able to walk to work provided me with the time I didn't believe I had for reflection and offered me quiet time and the space to do it. My mind wasn't always calm, but I had distance from external distractions, demands, and life's responsibilities.

This practice also forced me to breathe, both metaphorically and literally. I often needed to walk up and down hills, so my breath fluctuated. Too often, I've heard people say they don't have a moment to breathe, indicating a state of overwhelm, stress, and possibly distress. Breathwork—breathing patterns to support our mental, physical, and emotional well-being—helps promote relaxation, lower heart rate, and reduce blood pressure. Being more relaxed supports practicing mindfulness, and mindfulness allowed me to stay present in the discomfort of my thoughts as I reflected on racialized realities, my racial identity, and my engagement (or lack thereof) in antiracism efforts. Walking to work allowed me to absorb my new learnings and process the reality of what I didn't know, and it helped me metabolize more comprehensive truths and expand the space within myself for multiple truths, complexities, and nuances. Reflection helped me release binary ways of thinking.

I experienced many illuminations on these walks. I was able to accept that while I wanted to be good, due to socialized mindsets and behaviors I was not automatically a safe person for Black and Brown folks. But I still had to accept that what I wanted wasn't enough, that my words were not proof of my goodness or trustworthiness, that I would make mistakes, and that those mistakes would cause harm to others whether I was aware of it or not. I still had to accept that even if I developed deep, loving, and authentic relationships with Black and Brown folks, the likelihood of me disappointing them at some point was high. I also had to accept that I needed to change how I held myself accountable and how I apologized, that even if I offered a sincere apology, I was not entitled to it being accepted. And I had to accept that there was no "perfect" in antiracism and that I was imperfect. Letting go of perfection didn't mean I stopped trying or caring; it meant a mindset shift. I wanted to strive for excellence, understanding that I would make mistakes or miss the mark and that my impact and intent would not always align.

Another reality that my walks illuminated for me was that as a human being I had basic human needs. It might seem simple, silly, or obvious, but by not acknowledging my own needs, I wasn't taking care of myself. I was running from meeting to meeting and from one responsibility to the next. I'd grab a banana in the morning only to notice it was still sitting in the netted side pocket of my backpack when I got home, and I'd fill my water bottle in the morning to hydrate throughout the day only to realize it was still more than half full by the evening. And though I always hoped to get a good night's rest, I often lay awake in bed for hours worrying about what didn't go perfectly that day, cataloging everything I had to get done, or weaving worst-case scenario thoughts. By not caring for myself, my body didn't have what it needed to regulate my emotions, stabilize my thoughts, or be present in the moment. I needed to breathe, the kind of intentional, focused, slow, deep breathing that supports the nervous system, not the automatic breathing pattern of the lungs. I also needed to eat to energize myself throughout the day and reduce feelings of anxiety, as well as hydrate—our brains are mostly water, after all—to support my ability to think, focus, and stay alert. I needed shelter, a place to rest my head where I felt safe and relaxed so I could unwind and process my days, and I needed restful sleep to support my overall health, increase my attention span, and boost my memory and ability to learn new things.

On days when I hadn't eaten enough, drank enough water, or slept well, it was harder for me to unlearn and relearn; it was easier to lean into defensiveness or anger when I heard something I didn't like or hadn't learned beforehand. If I wanted to be present and listen to others' experiences, realities, or perspectives, I needed to take care of my basic human needs. By doing so, it was easier to be open to new information and to build and maintain healthy, authentic relationships. By taking care of myself, it became easier to accept being an imperfect human. Accepting my fallibility allowed me to hold myself accountable and be held accountable with greater ease and to recognize the harm my behavior had caused. It also allowed me to offer myself grace through mistakes, atonements, and learnings.

In 2011, while still working for the Seattle Office of Emergency Management, I began collaborating with a new employee in another department, Amica. Amica had recently moved to Seattle from Louisiana for her new role. I'd been on the hiring panel for the position and was thrilled about the opportunity to work with her. She's just a few years older than me, but our lives have been very different. She grew up and lived in the South her whole life before coming to Seattle. After having her first child when she was twenty and her second child a few years later, she navigated law school while raising both young children. She'd recently gotten married and was in discussions with her husband about expanding their family. Amica is Black. I was single, had recently come out to my family, was exploring my **gender identity** and discovering my creative side in community spaces, and am White. On paper we couldn't have been more different. In reality our values aligned and our openness to each other created the foundation for a decades-long collaborative relationship that feels more like a familial one.

One of my favorite memories of our relationship is an early interaction we had while sitting in the new Seattle Emergency Operations Center. After a levy almost a decade earlier funded its construction, the state-of-the-art center had recently opened and our office had just moved in. I was giving her a tour of the space when she stopped me with a curious, confused, and awestruck look and asked skeptically, "Did you have to scan your hand to open the door?"

"I did. It creeps me out a little, but originally they were going to put in a retinal scanner, and that would've felt worse," I shared.

Amica, tilting her head to the side, inquired, "Do you ever think the government creates these systems just to collect more info on employees?"

"Yes. I also think spending money on buildings, equipment, and the latest technology allows them to present an image of preparedness to the public that doesn't truly exist," I expanded.

Amica laughed and added, "So true." After a short pause, she continued, "Can I ask you something?"

I immediately answered, "Always."

"I heard you train police officers not to profile racially? Is that true?" I could hear the befuddled tone in her voice.

After a long exhale, all I could muster was, "Ish."

"What does that mean?" she asked with discernment.

After another long exhale, I replied, "Well, technically, I cofacilitate a training on the problems with race-based profiling."

"How is that different from what I said?" she asked directly.

"Training indicates that people are learning. That is not my experience of the training," I shared.

"What do you experience in the training?"

"For one, most of the people consider me an outsider because I'm not a sworn officer and therefore can't possibly understand anything related to policing. They also have more authority than I do and test every limit throughout the day. Participants often show up at the last minute, take their time talking to each other, and ignore requests from me or another facilitator to take their seats, finish their conversations, and be quiet. It's usually an indication of how the day will go. It's common for people to refuse to fill out their name cards, to read fully expanded newspapers, to fake snoring, or to whistle suspenseful theme music. It feels like facilitating a daycare, not a group of professionals."

"Seriously?!" Amica exclaimed.

"I wish I were kidding. It's hard. Really hard. Not the training—the training is pretty straightforward: watch a video, participate in a table discussion, engage in a large group discussion, or complete an activity; rinse and repeat.

The hard part is that participants often rip every video apart, discuss whatever they want at their tables, say absolutely nothing during the large group coversation, or throw a tantrum. We've had someone slide all the materials off our facilitator table, someone flip a table, and someone throw their chair, and we've had plenty of people scream obscenities at us during training or at the department. No matter what we try, a non-eventful training is rare," I elaborated.

Seeking clarification, Amica asked, "What do you mean 'no matter what we try'?"

I explained, "Most facilitators dropped out before the training series began. We started with thirty, but only six of us are left in the rotation. The remaining six include four people from the training unit and two civilian employees, Esme and me. We're all trainers and facilitators invested in constructive training and facilitation. We brainstorm often and try new ways to create an open and nonjudgmental space, to set the tone for the training and training space, and to increase participation."

To my surprise, Amica began to laugh out loud.

"What's so funny?" I asked.

"Casey," Amica said with the tone of a wise elder, "did you think those officers would want to learn how not to racially profile when most of them learned to do exactly that?" She offered this question in such a warm way, though I could tell she was fighting back her simultaneous laughter and anger.

After a pause, she continued, "The Slave Patrols[35] forged the roots of policing. Of course they racially profile. Of course they target Black and Brown people."

Feeling a little embarrassed for not knowing about the Slave Patrols, I said, "Honestly, I had hoped some of the younger officers, female officers, and non-White officers might engage in ways that support the conversation. They don't, but a number of them have followed up with me after trainings, thanking me or leaving me voicemails sharing their experiences with policing. I always ask why they didn't speak up during the training, because it would've been more powerful. The number one answer I get is that if they speak up, no one will have their backs. No one would respond, or they'd 'slow-roll' to an officer-in-need-of-assistance call."

"They're trying to survive in a culture that doesn't want to change," Amica said while shaking her head. "So what are you doing in there?"

I surprised myself by saying, "Surviving, continuing the conversation, and making way for those who come in after me."

It was at that moment that I fully acknowledged the relay efforts of antiracism work. Slave Patrols were created to suppress uprisings, resistance, and escape by enslaved

---

35. "The Origins of Modern Day Policing," NAACP, accessed June 16, 2024, https://naacp.org/find-resources/history-explained/origins-modern-day-policing.

people through fear, terror, excessive force, and policing. I was standing on the shoulders of those who resisted, spoke up, pushed back, protested, and advocated for societal and cultural change. I would not be a part of the last group of trainers, facilitators, or change agents; the work would continue, evolve, and expand regardless of any resistance to its need. The way the trainings were going was *not* a determination of my worth or value, nor were they an indicator of whether I was good or good enough. I wanted to facilitate dialogue, but as a facilitator I couldn't force anyone to engage. I couldn't make anyone behave like an adult or professionally, and I couldn't make anyone consider another perspective.

In that moment with Amica, I was also able to acknowledge my humanity, clarify my role's expectations, and recognize my connection to something so much bigger than myself. Recognizing my own humanity at a deeper level has helped me see humanity in others, including those with whom I don't always agree. I strive to bring this foundational moment with me when I work with anyone seeking a more equitable and antiracist society.

Those insights helped me in 2022 when I supported a public-serving national organization in advancing its DEI initiatives beyond feel-good activities such as lunch-and-learns and cultural celebration events. For decades, the organization struggled to retain its Black and Brown employees due to inequitable recruiting, hiring, and promotion practices that led to White people holding almost all supervisory, managerial, and leadership roles. Over the prior decade, the average retention rate was twelve years for White leaders, eight years for White supervisors and managers, and six years for White employees. The average rate for Black and Brown people, however, was approximately two years for leaders (with no more than one Black or Brown leader present at a time), four years for supervisors and managers, and eighteen months for employees.

I was invited in by the DEIBA committee, which consisted of five Black and Brown employees: a manager and a leader, two White administrative assistants, and the multiracial consultant the company had brought in a few years prior to support the establishment of the DEIBA infrastructure. When we first met, I asked them what they considered to be the most significant barrier to advancing the committee's work. Everyone agreed it was their White colleagues.

Donna, the manager, kicked off the responses with, "You gotta understand, Casey, we are a service organiza- tion. Everyone is here because of our mission to help those experiencing inequities in accessing healthcare. We are theoretically heart- and mission-driven."

I often hear this in purpose-driven organizations.

"All the White people here think they can't be racist because they care about healthcare and want to support everyone having access to quality and affordable healthcare," said Layla, the youngest employee on the committee, who worked for Donna. All the heads bobbed up and down around the table.

"So, other White people are racist, but not them?" I asked (stated).

"Oh, God, one thousand percent," affirmed Tanesha, another employee.

Sinclair, the consultant, added, "Casey, I'm tired. *We* are tired."

Sounds of agreement ("Mmm-hmm" and "You can say that again") and sharp exhales rumbled around the room.

"Of course you are," I said. "In what ways can I be of support in reaching the White people here?"

"Well, I don't know that you can reach them," said Lashay, the only Black or Brown leader at the organization. "But you can certainly give us a break from repeating ourselves, being asked to validate their 'wokeness,' continuing to go unheard, and experiencing the same shit from them."

I affirmed, "I want to be able to do that. Will y'all share with me what work has been done and any common forms of resistance you've experienced? I'd love to both amplify your past work, reinforce it, and build on it. By 'building on it,' I mean, what do you want me to say or bring up so you don't have to say or repeat it? I can name things that will be hard for them to hear, and I can take the blame if there's a revolt."

Sinclair asked, "Are you willing to be the 'bad guy' so we don't have to be called 'the angry Black woman' or the 'problem Woman of Color'?"

"Absolutely," I responded.

A small smile appeared on Donna's face before she asked, "Will you talk with them about their racism?"

"I can," I offered, "and I can talk about what I thought racism was, how my beliefs and ideas were challenged, the discomfort in that, why our comfort can't be centered, and anything else you want me to weave in."

Even with years of experience, deep relationships, and countless moments of reckoning under my belt, I still stumble. The success of this project depends on who you ask. Leadership was triggered by my use of the terms, "White privilege" and "White fragility." These leaders did what many do when they bump into a growing edge: they disengaged. This always harms any equity efforts being made. The Black and Brown employees felt relief at not having to be the person coaching leadership or navigating their resistance. My time with this organization reminded me that no amount of commitment or experience immunizes us from making mistakes or causing harm. Despite my intentions, there are moments when I miss the mark—when my words land wrong, when I misread a dynamic, when I lean too hard into urgency or not enough into trust.

This work isn't about achieving flawlessness, though. It's about staying in it, especially when it's messy. As you'll soon learn, I've made some missteps even in recent years, and I've been called out, challenged, and reminded that being engaged in antiracism work doesn't mean you stop making mistakes. It means you stay willing to learn from them.

Chapter 12

A FRIENDSHIP I LOST, AND THE LESSON I WILL NEVER FORGET

Practicing Antiracism Is Not a Destination but an Evolution

One of my most soul-crushing regressions cost me a dear friend, Riadel.

Riadel was one of the most remarkable people I'd ever met, but I was in awe of them before we met. I'd seen them at many queer community events, and they always stood out to me. I first noticed their laughter, one of those deep, infectious belly laughs that brought smiles to anyone around them. They also had a unique style, incorporating flourishes into their outfits such as robust hair fasteners, bold earrings, and glitter nail polish. They radiated excitement and always had people lining up to talk to them. I'd seen Riadel MC at multiple events, and they consistently ensured that people felt included and as safe as possible in a community environment. They were quick with their jokes and comebacks.

Riadel was an abolitionist and Filipina. When I had the chance to meet them, first in a community writing class and then at an RSJI Community Council meeting, I felt fortunate. I felt lucky to get to know someone so dynamic, so mindful, and who was such a serious badass. They were kind and funny but also fierce, calling out racist, sexist, homophobic, fatphobic, and ableist talk and behaviors immediately, firmly, and often with great charm. We developed a fast, intimate, platonic relationship full of play, laughter, and raw conversations about everything, including our trauma histories. I went from being a fan of Riadel to wholly loving and cherishing them. Years later, after our friendship had deepened, I fucked it all up.

We were out to dinner when, after they shared a story, I asked, "You're a US citizen, right?"

I knew they were a US citizen! I knew where they were born in the US, I knew precisely where in the US their parents had been born, and I'd heard their family immigration story many times. I'd also heard about the pain and hurt from anti-Asian and anti-immigrant hate that their family had experienced throughout generations. After all we'd shared together and the intimacy we'd developed, it was an egregious microaggression on my part. I had the opportunity at that moment to take ownership of my offense; there was space for me to own it—we both stopped talking and were frozen with our forks in the air—and we both knew what had just happened. But I didn't own what I did or even acknowledge it. I started talking as if nothing had occurred.

At that moment, I convinced myself that if I just moved on, everything would be okay. Of course that wasn't true. The rest of the dinner was uncomfortable. Riadel quickly asked for a to-go box and kept checking their phone, and I kept acting as if nothing had happened.

When I got back to my apartment, I dove down multiple shame spirals: *I am such an asshole! Why did I say that?! What is fucking wrong with me? Shit, shit, shit. Now everyone's going to know what a racist asshole I am.*

Panicked, I cowardly decided to text Riadel an apology in a casual tone, hoping for immediate absolution: "Hi friend. Sorry I asked that question about your citizenship. I know you're a US citizen. That was so weird."

They texted back, "Okay." I then let myself off the hook thinking that the apology I offered was sufficient for the harm and heartache I'd caused them.

Over the following weeks, I continued to text them as if nothing had happened. They sometimes responded with a thumbs up or a "Haha," but eventually they stopped responding altogether. Our friendship was over. We never had another one-on-one hangout again.

It broke my heart to lose that friendship, and it was all my fault. I not only said something racist, rude, ignorant, and harmful, but then I blew it off as if it wasn't a big deal when it was really a huge deal. I also focused on how *I* felt: I centered my experience of that exchange and my fear of how others would perceive me, and I offered a pitiful apology, expecting that to be enough. Riadel deserved better from me, a close and trusted friend. They deserved an authentic and meaningful apology, one that centered on *their* experience of that moment and *their* feelings. They deserved my humility, my self-accountability, and the vulnerable honesty of me owning my words and the harm those words caused. They deserved to hear about my commitment to not doing that again, reflecting on my behavior, and holding myself accountable.

I understand how and why I broke their trust and how I minimized that moment and their experience of it. I understand that, more than the initial harm I caused, it was the lack of my accountability that made me an unsafe person for them to be in a deep relationship with. And I recognize that the pain I felt in losing that relationship was nothing compared to the pain I caused Riadel.

It was a genuinely humble moment for me to witness my Whiteness ruining one of my most cherished friendships.

I was horrified by what I'd said to Riadel; that was a mistake, and mistakes inevitably happen. But the lasting damage came from not addressing it in the moment, prioritizing my own comfort over their experience, offering a hollow apology, not allowing space for them to share their experience of the harm, and moving on as if nothing had occurred.

Mistakes are a part of antiracism work. No one expects perfection. However, antiracism work expects meaningful accountability, authentic vulnerability, continuous learning, and evolving growth. Something I learned from losing my friendship with Riadel is that a genuine apology centers on the harmed person and their experience.

As I began to practice accountability in a new way, I created a formula. The intent wasn't to ensure that my apology was always accepted but that my apology was meaningful to the person receiving it. I call this a "Justice Apology," which includes four actions:

1. Apologize for the harm experienced.
2. Thank the person for sharing with you, and acknowledge the emotional labor it took to share.
3. Name what you will do differently and how you will be held accountable.
4. Move forward.

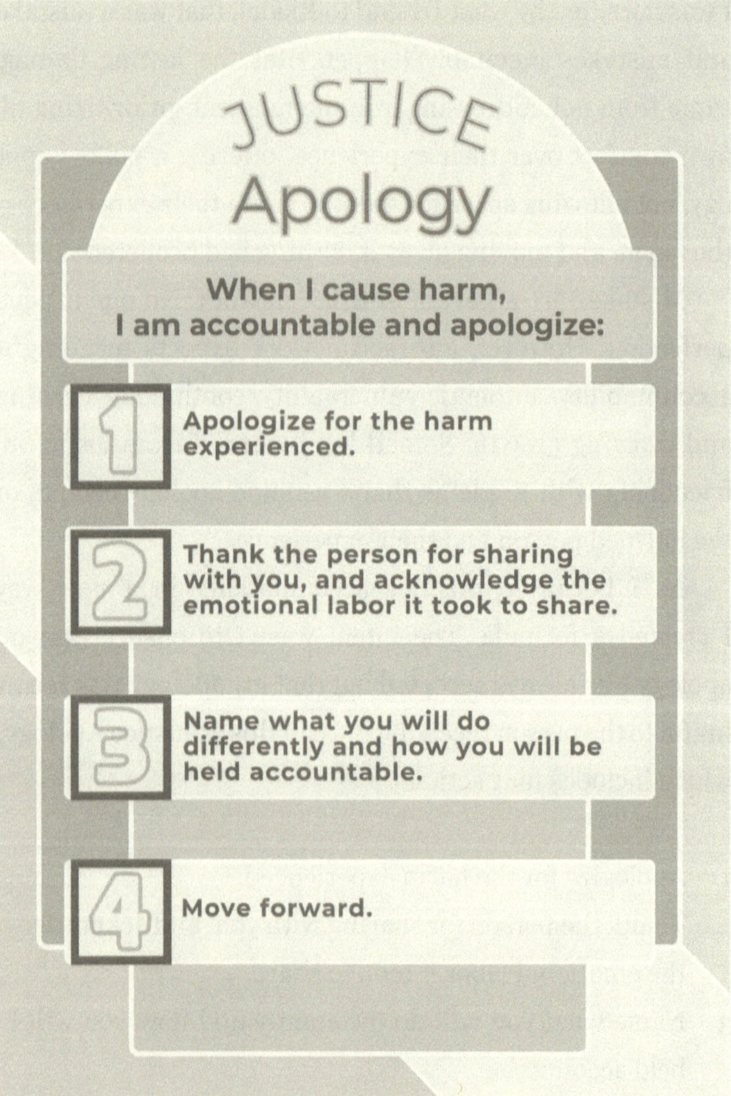

JUSTICE
Apology
When I cause harm,
I am accountable and apologize:
1 Apologize for the harm experienced.
2 Thank the person for sharing with you, and acknowledge the emotional labor it took to share.
3 Name what you will do differently and how you will be held accountable.
4 Move forward.

Figure 5

In tandem with strengthening my apologies, I also had to find ways to process my shame, fear, and guilt without burdening the person I'd harmed. Two such practices I rely on most are talking with friends who support my antiracism journey and journaling. These practices support me in releasing feelings from my body while maintaining a sense of connection and having a dedicated space for nonjudgmental processing.

Several events in my life have helped me develop the ability to accept my imperfections and practice meaningful accountability. Before I came out to my family, my biggest fear was being banished from my church due to my **sexual orientation**. My prayers throughout the day consisted of apologizing to God for my thoughts and feelings and begging him to make me straight. My secret grew so big inside me that I felt like I was going to burst. I desperately suppressed any inklings to blurt it out, because I knew that once it was out, there was no going back. I knew the consequences. I knew my family would disown me, that I'd be a disappointment and embarrassment to my parents, that I wouldn't be allowed back into my church. I knew I would be on my own and alone in a new way. I wanted to die. My only obstacle was that suicide was also a sin and an abomination.

One night, the fear and bursting sensations in my body drove me thirty miles away from home to a church where I didn't know anyone. I ran through the colossal, dark brown doors as if my shoes were on fire and the church was the last reserve of water. It was a small church designed to accommodate approximately 250 people for worship and looked very similar to the one I attended. Extraordinary stained-glass windows gleamed throughout the space, illuminating the high ceilings. I passed one pew after the other, shuffling along the 1970s-style carpet. I wanted to be close to the altar crucifix, to be close to God. I side-stepped into the second pew and sat down, not yet knowing what I was going to do. There was only one other person in the church, an older woman kneeling in front of the votive candles, her head bent into her hands held in prayer. I felt overwhelmed by shame and self-loathing as I collapsed to my knees and began to pray. It was the same prayer I'd practiced with increasing frequency: pleading with God to make my queerness not true. After a few moments, I burst into tears. I didn't show a lot of emotion at this point in my life, keeping a stoic disposition. My weeping became increasingly pronounced, tears poured down my face, my body began to convulse from the release of the terror I was holding inside, and my breath shortened and sped up. This went on for a while.

In Catholicism, the priests and nuns serve as the medium between you and God, shepherding your relationship with him. Before he even arrived, I felt a priest approaching to sit next to me, and when he did I felt despondent. Crying offered a small release from the exhaustion of holding the secret, but once that tension eased, I was left with a deeper, emptier sadness. After some time passed, he asked if I was okay in a quiet, gentle tone.

I looked up at him from my kneeling position and said with my thick New York accent, "Father, forgive me, I mean no disrespect, but do I look okay to you?" He smiled, nodded his head, and we sat quietly again for an extended amount of time.

Eventually, he broke the silence. "Do you want to talk about it?" I shook my head and burst into tears again. He placed his hand on my shoulder and gave it a gentle squeeze. "What don't you want to talk about? What's weighing on you, my child?"

I pushed myself up to sit next to him on the pew. "I'm sorry, Father, I can't," I said. My crying had become so heavy that I was heaving, gasping for breath between sniffles and tears. "I can't speak it, Father. I can't say it because if I say it it'll be true and then my life is over." He held my hand. We sat silently again for a long time.

He again broke the silence by asking in his thick New York accent, "Do you want the bottom line?"

I hadn't known that was an option and was dumbstruck. "Okay," I said.

He sat up straight and firmly and turned to face me. I mirrored his movements. "Don't be an asshole," he said. "Don't be an asshole to other people, and don't be an asshole to yourself. If you stick with that, you're gonna be okay."

Inside, I thought, *That's it! That's it! I can do that.* I leaped from my seat to hug him. "Thank you, Father. Thank you. I think you just saved my life."

He hugged me back and said, "Lucky me."

After that, he stood up and told me to take my time. As he walked away, I realized we never exchanged names.

This moment changed me. The weight of hating myself for years, of believing I was a mistake, of feeling lost, of believing I was destined for hell and likely dragging my family down with me, lifted. This moment provided a salve to the anguish I'd been experiencing on the inside. At a cellular level, I suddenly felt a sense of grotesqueness, like my inner self was sabotaging who I was supposed to become. This moment set the foundation for how I wanted to exist in this world without the brain spirals of shame I'd practiced over my lifetime. My breath slowed, my tears stopped, and a sense of ease and peace washed over me. I was still afraid to tell my family I was queer, but I felt safer from eternal damnation. I also felt comforted by the belief that how I interacted with and treated others, as well as myself, was more important than who I was attracted to. This moment allowed me to have faith without being strictly bound to religion, and thankfully it liberated me from the belief that I was an abomination, a mistake, tempted by the devil, or better off dead. Healing the wounds my religion inflicted took longer than I wished—and often involved unexpected people, like that priest.

A few short years later, after I'd met with the priest but before ruining my friendship with Riadel, Massachusetts became the first state to legalize gay marriage, and I was living in Washington State. One Saturday afternoon, I was sitting in my apartment exploring the neighborhood newspaper for things to do, and I came across a movie called *For the Bible Tells Me So.* Based on the description alone, which stated that the film explored the perceived conflict between Christianity and homosexuality, I went to see the documentary in a Seattle theater in the University District. Once I had my ticket in hand and walked into the theater, I paused and thought, *What the hell am I doing?* I wondered whether I'd made a huge mistake by choosing a movie rooted in hate and shame about a part of myself.

The theater was dimly lit with around twenty people spread out across the space. For every filled seat, there were at least two empty seats on either side, and there was a palpable tension of uncertainty and fear among the patrons in the theater. I sat in the center, with an older woman in her late sixties sitting two seats to my left, her coat on and her purse clutched in her lap. We nodded at each other quickly and then immediately shifted away our gazes. I focused on the seatback in front of me and could feel my heart start to race as the previews began. Without realizing it, I'd clinched my jaw and fists. I could feel the panic, rooted in my hypervigilance, washing over me. *Just breathe,*

I reminded myself—something my new therapist said to do when I noticed my panic rising. *This is stupid*, I thought as every cell in my body screamed for me to run to safety. *I'm trying new tools for my new life, not old tools from my old life*, I told myself as I tried to calm down. *Breathe. Slowly breathe in, slowly breathe out. You can leave at any time. You can leave the moment the film gets church-creepy.* I took a few more slow, deep breaths with my eyes (close to) closed while the last trailer played.

To my surprise and delight, the film featured several religious leaders and scholars, individuals of faith who'd come out, and family members of those who had. The religious leaders and scholars shared details of the Bible I didn't remember reading and my church sermons had never focused on, such as how Leviticus 11:12 says eating shellfish is a sin and how Genesis 38 indicates that the pull-out method as contraception is a sin punishable by death. These religious scholars explained that it was essential to read the Bible's text with an understanding of the cultural context of the time, given that the Old and New Testaments were written over centuries by men in different cultural contexts. For example, they described how Leviticus 15:28 discusses at length that discharges causing uncleanliness, including wet dreams and menstruation, are unholy and that being cleansed by a priest requires animal sacrifice in addition to extended isolation. These were not things discussed or practiced in our church.

A light bulb went off in my mind: not everything written thousands of years ago needed to be taken literally. As obvious as this may seem now, it was a radical thought for me at the time based on all my years of conditioning. Although there are a few Christian-identified churches that select lines from the Bible and take them literally, no church takes every line of the Bible literally. Have you seen the crusade against the shellfish industry? Animal sacrifices after wet dreams or menstruation? Laws criminalizing men who pull out before ejaculation? Me neither.

The most powerful parts of the film were the personal stories shared. Only a few participants experienced immediate acceptance of their sexuality. Some experienced various stages of self- and relationship-repair, healing, and acceptance, and others experienced absolutely devastating rejection. An older mom shared the story of her inability to accept her daughter when she came out, reading parts of a letter from her daughter written shortly before she committed suicide. Suicide was one of my greatest fears for myself. My chest tightened and my fingers gripped the armrests. Before the story could fully sink in, I heard the older woman next to me burst into tears. She bent her head forward to meet the handkerchief she pulled from her purse, and I heard the pain in her sobs as she struggled to quiet her breathing. Without thinking, I extended my left hand to her, palm up. The moment she realized my offer was for her, she grabbed my hand with intensity, then looked at me and whispered, "I did that. I did that to my son." I wondered whether my parents would've been in her position had I not had that lifesaving conversation with the priest and chosen suicide instead. My heart sank at the thought of the pain my death might have caused them. Tears welled in my eyes as I laid my right hand on top of hers and wordlessly moved to sit beside her. We held hands for the rest of the film.

At the end of the film, she told me she now "fights like hell" so that no parent or child has to experience the pain of a parent's rejection or a child's suicide. We embraced, holding each other tightly, understanding we were surrogates for each other. I saw similar embraces occurring around the theater. Before long, the whole theater had convened in the center of the room, holding hands and hugging one another. We told each other that we were loved and that we weren't alone. This experience was like an antiseptic tincture: painful, but necessary, clearing the way for me to grieve both the loss of my religion and the seismic rift my coming out caused in my family.

In that moment, I realized that I might not have felt a sense of belonging in my family, but I did belong. My family might not have accepted me, but I was accepted. I might not have felt loved by my family, but I was loved. I realized that acceptance and community save lives. I did not need to be perfect to have belonging. That said, to be a part of healthy community and relationships requires accountability.

Chapter 13

WORKING TOWARD EMBODIED ANTIRACISM

Letting My Body Lead Me to Braver Conversations, Harder Truths, and Real Growth

Many of us have been socialized and conditioned to think our way through life, relying only on our conscious brains and minds. When we do this, we miss all the information our bodies are trying to give us to help us stay safe and rooted.

An example of this is how even seemingly innocuous learning can have long-term, unhealthy consequences. I was raised to always answer the question, "How ya doing?" with, "Good," "Great," or "Fine," no matter what was going on in my life or how I felt. At a certain point, I stopped naming my feelings at all, even to myself. In my childhood home, my parents encouraged us to put on happy faces as we left our front door in order to be seen as a normal, happy, and good family. This equated to fake smiles, withholding reality from others, and suppressing all emotions that challenged our family facade.

Suppressing feelings also meant not learning healthy ways to process a wide range of emotions. My mother was often angry in our home, which usually resulted in verbal, emotional, and physical abuse. The message I absorbed was that being angry leads to violence, so if I didn't want to be violent, I couldn't let myself feel angry. For decades I never allowed myself to feel anger. I was angry, but I didn't know how to sit with it, allow myself to dissect the causes of it, or process it in a healthy way. Not understanding how to acknowledge and process my anger contributed to my feelings of hypervigilance. I operated from a fight, flight, freeze, and fawn mindset, always on the lookout for perceived or actual threats and thinking about how I would prevent, stop, avoid, or counter them. The anxiety and depression I developed because of this practice severely diminished my willingness to take risks.

My years of long, challenging justice work helped me not only process the reality of racism but also begin to reconnect with my body. Learning how my body responded in uncomfortable but physically safe situations allowed me to recognize which emotions I was experiencing. I learned how to name my feelings to myself and how to share them with others. I also learned what I needed to process and how to take care of myself in a new way. My anxiety masked many emotions, including sadness, frustration, hurt, and uneasiness. Learning to recognize that each of those underlying feelings actually manifested distinctly in my body was transformative and empowering. My energy used to tank when I felt sad. Though that's still true, now I can name it and ask for what I need, such as alone time or time with a close friend. I used to belittle myself, hide, and avoid people I felt had hurt me. Now I do something to move the hurt through my body, such as take a bath, go to yoga, or listen to music. I also practice deciphering the distinction between the facts of the situation, the emotions I'm feeling, and the thoughts in my mind, an exercise that allows me to address the cause of the hurt and test my conclusions against reality. Reconnecting with my body and listening to how it reacts allows me to process my emotions more consciously and in line with my values. I feel empowered to take risks, and risk-taking is required in antiracism work.

In 2020, I was supporting a mid-sized affordable housing consultant firm to help them advance DEI efforts beyond a company statement and an employee affinity group. I had the opportunity to meet with leadership multiple times to hear about their DEI successes. I also met with the HR manager and her team to discuss what had been done in the past, the approaches that had worked in supporting deeper dialogue, and the challenges they foresaw. Finally, I met with each employee who was part of the affinity group and attended an affinity group meeting myself. There weren't many surprises. Leadership believed they were succeeding in advancing equity based on their intentions rather than outcomes. Their focus remained on revenue-generating strategies, cutting overhead costs, maintaining operational efficiency, and sustaining a polished public image. While they were thinking about DEI, their actions often failed to align with the deeper cultural shifts needed for equity to take root. HR found itself caught in the crossfire—pressured by industry regulations, constrained by leadership's priorities, and burdened by employee dissatisfaction. The HR employees were thinking about DEI, too, but often felt paralyzed by the tension between what they wanted to do and what they were permitted or resourced to do. Meanwhile, employees were experiencing the organization's DEI efforts as hollow and performative; many felt overworked, unheard, and disillusioned by the lack of meaningful change. Despite this, they were the ones doing the most reflective and emotionally taxing work: grappling with mistrust, voicing their truths, and striving to build an environment that lived up to the organization's stated values. They also carried the deepest disappointment because they held the greatest hope that DEI efforts might finally bring equity into their daily work lives, close the gaps in opportunity, and realign the imbalanced expectations between them and their leaders.

At the first company-wide all-staff meeting I attended, the Black and Brown affinity group shared a video highlighting national and company-wide race-based inequities, including the demographics of leadership versus those of their frontline employees. They then shared substantial disparities in company retention rates based on racial identities. The video also featured employees sharing real-life examples of microaggressions they'd experienced while working at the company. It was powerful.

When the video ended, the meeting host said, "Wow, wow. Thanks for sharing that. It's good for us all to keep in mind." He then proceeded to talk about his hunger level and how he was looking forward to lunch. After a brief, uncomfortable laugh by the host and a few people sitting in the crowd, he began to review Q1 wins and what to expect for the remainder of the year.

I could feel the discomfort in my body. I felt disappointed in the host for not commenting on the video after such vulnerable public sharing by the Black and Brown employees. I felt a pit in my stomach thinking about how the members of the affinity group must have felt at that moment. And I felt annoyed at leadership for not speaking up when the video concluded. My annoyance manifested in me fidgeting in my seat and making unusual facial expressions. As my breath got shorter and faster, my heartbeat faster, and my cheeks heated, I recognized these as indicators that it was time to use my voice.

"Pardon me," I said, standing up while raising my hand and taking a deep breath.

"Oh, Casey. Great, hi. For those who are unfamiliar, Casey will be supporting some of our upcoming DEI efforts. The floor is yours," the meeting host invited.

"Hi, everyone," I started. "I want to acknowledge that powerful video we just saw from the affinity group. I'm sorry y'all have had to experience those microaggressions. I want to thank you for being so vulnerable and courageous in sharing some of those experiences with us. And I want to assure you that I will do my best to avoid causing you further harm. That said, I am human, I make mistakes, and I am always learning. Please know that I will be open to feedback, correction, and new ways of engaging that support our ability to build trust."

As soon as I finished, members of the leadership team were jumping all over themselves to repeat my words before the meeting continued. This moment provided the most significant insight into where the company and leaders really were in their DEI work.

After the meeting, leadership swarmed around me. Some thanked me for speaking up, while others wanted to know whether I thought what they were saying was okay. A few said, "We have some work to do," looking at other particular leaders, implying they were the problem. None of these behaviors are uncommon in an organization; most leaders want to be seen not just as "on board" with DEI work but as people who truly "get it." However, behaviors like that of the meeting host are reactionary and hurtful. In moments like these, leaders often speak up in service of their self-perception as being good people.

I'm not always as fully embodied as I was in that particular moment, but the more I practice listening to and connecting with my body, the more I'm able to show up in my desired state for conversations about racial justice.

Embodiment is the connection between our minds (our thoughts), our hearts (our emotions), and our hands (the behaviors we show or the actions we take). It allows us to name the feelings we're experiencing, to know how those feelings are showing up in our bodies, and to choose how we want to respond. When we, as White people, can engage from an embodied antiracism state, we are more willing to speak out against racism. By practicing presence, we increase our ability to stay with the discomfort of addressing racism rather than avoid it. The more we sit with discomfort, the more equipped we are to do meaningful antiracism work, including reflecting on our internalized, unconscious beliefs. As we deepen our self-awareness through that reflection, we build greater courage to confront racism in ourselves and in the world.

Embodiment helps us accept our imperfections and grow through mistakes. And when we engage from an embodied state, we create more opportunities to connect across differences, strengthen our relationships, and operate in solidarity across racial lines.

Chapter 14

NO ONE HAS ALL THE ANSWERS

Practicing Antiracism with Humility, Reflection, and Relational Accountability

There is no one way to work on becoming or being antiracist, nor is there a quick fix or magical wand to get there. This is why I continually strive for antiracism and call myself experienced, not an expert. Constantly examining the racism embedded in us and standing in solidarity with Black and Brown leadership and community takes meaningful commitment and requires exploring our racialized individual and national histories. We must develop an understanding of the societal creation of a preference for Whiteness. We must discover who we are as people without embedded racism. And we must evolve along with our language and the tools we use in these efforts.

It's important to establish and commit to your personal antiracism goals and to honor where you are in your antiracism journey. You may be new to antiracism, you may be less racist than your relatives and not know where to start, or you may be a solidarity partner or a racial justice organizer or champion. No matter where you are in this movement, you are needed. Remember that there is always more to learn and there are always growth and engagement opportunities. You will make mistakes—you are human. What matters most is how you respond to, engage with, and grow from those mistakes.

While I've had the privilege of intentionally engaging in antiracism work since my mid-twenties, entirely new generations have grown up since then and are now leading a multitude of racial and social justice efforts. We must be willing to learn from them. Last year, I attended a networking event with some of my collaborators. I shared what I thought was a funny YouTube video that I'd used in an intersectional solidarity training when discussing bystander intervention. The video shows several people in a café: a young gentleman is working behind the counter, a rushed woman on her phone is placing her order, another woman is working on her computer with papers spread across the table, a young gay couple is sitting side-by-side at a table sharing pancakes, and a young heterosexual couple is sitting by the window, furthest away from the counter. The video introduces each character and then pans to the straight couple in front of the window. The man expresses delight in his pancakes and offers some to the woman at the table with him. She declines this invitation. He persists and extends his arm with a fork full of pancake in her direction. The woman leans back, starts looking at her phone, and waves the pancakes away. The others in the café notice; some look at each other while others turn and distract themselves. The man by the window continues to push his pancakes at the woman until he begins to tap his syrupy pancakes on the woman's cheek. Finally, the woman working at the table stands up and tells the man to stop, yelling, "Nobody wants your pancakes, man!" The other patrons begin nodding and smiling at the woman who spoke up.

I found the video light and funny, and I wanted to share it as a resource for my collaborators to use to spark conversation in groups they might be facilitating. One of my younger colleagues standing next to me tilted her head and shifted her eyes to the ceiling corner, a look on her face like she was doing long division. "That's not funny. That's violent," she said.

Feeling surprised, confused, and curious, I asked, "What do you mean?"

She elaborated, "The woman at the window said 'no' multiple times. The guy continued to push his pancakes at her until he was assaulting her with them. And for most of the video, nobody did anything. It just feels like making light of domestic violence and rape culture."

I'd be lying if I didn't admit that my head spun and it took me a minute to process her words. My body froze.

I take pride in being a consent-oriented individual, and I've experienced domestic violence and never want to make light of any form of abuse.

After a few moments of awkward silence, I nodded and looked her in her eyes. "You're right," I said. "It's not a good video to use. My generation didn't learn to be as conscious of consent as your generation. I didn't learn about having and respecting boundaries until adulthood. Thank you for saying something. I never want to indicate my approval of or 'okayness' with domestic violence behaviors nor that a person's 'no' can be ignored. I'm grateful you and your peers won't stand for the shit we were taught to tolerate and accept. The video is gone." We then continued with our evening, moving past the moment.

Witnessing individuals become aware, activated, and engaged in a more profound and committed way has kept me in the work and motivated me to continue fighting for racial justice. While working for the Seattle Office for Civil Rights, it was common for participants who'd attended an RSJI training to reach out and ask to connect: "Hi Casey. I was in [XYZ] training last year. I'm wondering if I could take you up on your offer to have coffee?" Even if they reached out months or even years later, the answer was always yes!

One day after receiving such a message, I showed up at a small, hidden coffee shop downtown, expecting to meet with a woman named Darla. I facilitated hundreds of trainings per year for the city, so I didn't know what she looked like. I scanned the room but didn't see any solo women. While I enjoyed meeting people outside of the workplace because it allowed for more authentic and casual conversations, there was always a thought in the back of my mind that it might be a setup or a trap by my mother or someone who didn't support RSJI work. Relief washed over me as I saw a hand go up and wave me over.

Darla looked to be in her early thirties, and she presented as serious and organized with her notepad, laptop, and cellphone laid out. She was sitting with two young men, both of whom looked to be in their late twenties or early thirties. One of them, Ben, had a wide, full smile, and the other, Dan, appeared painfully shy. After our initial greetings, Darla sprang into explaining why the three of them wanted to meet with me, her sense of urgency seeping through each word: "We are all new employees, and each of us has attended at least one of the RSJI trainings. It's so clear to us that our coworkers and supervisors don't care about equity." Her underlying frustration was immediately clear.

Ben and Dan remained silent, nodding their heads and looking between Darla, me, and the table. Encouragingly I offered, "Let's slow down a little." This statement disoriented each of them in different ways. Darla, surprised, leaned back and crossed her arms. Ben's smile dissipated to near extinction. Dan tilted his head to the left. I continued,

"I want to hear about the behaviors you're experiencing and witnessing that give you the impression that your colleagues and supervisors don't care about equity. First, tell me a little bit about yourselves, your roles, and your prior racial equity work."

I could see the realization wash over them that we did not know each other, had no relationship, and shared no common context. We needed to establish a stronger foundation before strategizing and problem-solving. We shared our diverse backgrounds, the paths that led us to our respective roles at the city, and our histories of engaging in antiracism work. Even though we were only roughly ten years apart, there was a distinct generational gap that exposed the differences in our baseline antiracism analysis. When I was in primary school, racism was taught as something of the past, and though in college I could take classes dedicated to racialized history, the internet didn't take off until I was out of college, so my real learning about racism in the US didn't begin until my mid-twenties. For these three folks, racialized realities of the day were in the news and discussed in their middle school history classes. They learned about Black and Brown historical figures throughout the school year, and they had their own laptops in high school to do their own research, with access to a lot more information. At the time of our meeting, I'd been involved in antiracism work for more than ten years. This was Darla, Ben, and Dan's first experience of moving beyond an intellectual understanding of antiracism and into the practice of antiracism. Our shared commonality was being White people and wanting an end to racial injustice.

Darla let out a strong exhale before sharing, "That was nice. I feel more at ease." Ben and Dan nodded in agreement.

I smiled and said, "And it only took fifteen minutes. So, talk to me about what's going on at work."

Dan leaned in and in his low, soft voice, began, "There's a lot of tension in our office. Leadership talks about equity and being committed to equity, but it just isn't a practice. Our Black and Brown colleagues are exhausted, frustrated, and frankly, pissed."

Darla added, "For example, leadership talks all the time to staff, reporters, and the city council about their inclusive recruiting practices of tapping into the high schools, community colleges, and working with Black and Brown community nonprofits. That said, they almost never hire anyone from those funnels. To make it worse, all but one internal promotion has gone to a White employee over a Black or Brown employee."

Sadly, talk without action and inequitable promotion practices are common behaviors. I asked, "What has been done to call this out or hold leadership accountable?"

Ben chimed in, "All our staff meetings end with leadership either dismissing, ignoring, or yelling at our Black or Brown colleagues who speak."

"What do y'all do in those meetings?" I asked.

"We listen, agree, and support our Black and Brown colleagues," Darla shared proudly.

"How?" I asked. The table got quiet. I let the silence linger for a few seconds before asking, "Do you speak up in meetings? Check in on your colleagues after they've been dismissed, ignored, or yelled at by the boss? Ask your colleagues what support from you might look like? Have a one-on-one conversation with your boss expressing your frustration with the recruiting funnel or lack of diversity within leadership?"

More silence.

I saw all three shrinking, not knowing what to say. Breaking the tension, I offered, "No one is asking you to fix this." It was a message I'd needed to hear myself more than once. "You know it's wrong and creates a bad work environment. You wouldn't be here otherwise. Consider these questions: How do you show solidarity with your colleagues who've been advocating and fighting for equity? What can you do to lift their message? How can you take some of the heat off them? What resources are available to you?"

Dan excitedly jumped in: "We have an equity group within our department!" I then asked whether they'd reached out to them, and they replied they hadn't.

Dan offered to reach out and see how the group could support their work, and Ben said, "I can talk to a colleague whose cubicle is near mine. Sometimes they cry after those meetings. I'll ask her how I can support her in those meetings."

Finally, Darla added, "I need to think about why I reached out to you instead of talking with my colleagues who've been carrying the weight of this conversation."

It was an awareness moment for each of them, in different ways.

A few key takeaways for the three of them were that they didn't need to start by transforming leadership's mindset or ensuring that policies and practices were aligned. They needed to start with relationships, to connect with those already doing the work within their department.

A few years later, Darla became a colead of the department's equity group, and Dan became a volunteer with the RSJI program, serving as a trainer and facilitator for the race-based caucus. Ben, with his infamous smile, refused to take a promotion until leadership reflected the demographics of the staff.

One analogy I like to use for the antiracism development spectrum is gardening. Some people have no interest in gardening, while others are curious but unsure where to begin. Some are scouting where to grow, while others are just starting to churn the soil. Some are planting seeds and mapping out a growth plan, while others are watering, tending, or preparing to harvest. There are those who've been gardening for years but still struggle to produce and others with thriving gardens. Some keep to themselves, and some grow abundant gardens and generously share their yield, helping others along the way. We don't need to be in the same stage to grow together, and not every seed sprouts at the same time, or at all. Understanding that is essential to this work.

Several years ago, I was mindful of this analogy when supporting an organization in developing its strategic and inclusive community engagement approaches to reach a wider audience and coaching its leadership to assist with their buy-in on these new approaches. The coaching focused on expanding thinking around outreach, engagement, and connecting with others across differences. It was a largely White organization with a successful forty-year history and a median leadership age of fifty-four. They had a template for what they did, it got them work, and they were very committed to it. A sticking point for us in our collaboration was the recognition that their template succeeded only for a particular group of people: White, middle-class, suburban, college-educated women. And most of the leadership reflected those demographics. They assumed they just needed access to other demographics and that their template would continue to work brilliantly as it had before. I tried explaining to them that if they didn't know the lived experiences, realities, norms, or culture of their audience, it would be harder to reach them meaningfully. I also explained that since they wouldn't be starting from a baseline of trust, they'd need to build trust with these communities before the communities would engage with them authentically.

One day, one of the leaders with whom I had the least amount of engagement called me to her office. Marielle was in her late thirties and was massively overworked and visibly stressed. As a result of her overwhelm, she spoke tersely and often harshly. Her office was small with pale yellow walls and barely fit her desk, monitor, laptop, and chair; I had to pull in a chair for our impromptu meeting, and the back legs stuck out of the doorway. Marielle had largely avoided interacting with me, so I was curious to discover what she wanted to discuss. She presented a stoic expression steeped in exhaustion, the command of a leadership role, and annoyance. With her hands clasped in front of her and her forearms on her desk, she took a long inhale through her nose and then looked into my eyes as if my humanity had evaporated, her eyes like lasers. Then she began to speak: "I hear you think we don't do community outreach right?"

In my experience, phrases that start with "I hear you think" are an indicator that the other person is gearing up for an argument, usually one they plan to "win." I often like to get more information before reacting, so I gently inquired, "Marielle, wait. Can we back up a little? What are you hearing?"

Leaning back in her chair with a subtle huff, she said, "I've heard from my colleagues that you've been questioning how we do community outreach and are critical of our approach." Her vocal inflections oozed frustration.

Nodding in agreement and still curious, I replied, "Ish, Marielle. That's why you hired me—to support expanding your outreach and engagement approaches to reach more people and communities. I understand that y'all have been doing community outreach for a long time and that, in a way, it has been very successful. The approach y'all have created works well for White, middle-class, suburban communities. I'm here because I was under the impression y'all wanted to expand the communities you can reach, engage with, and build relationships with."

She closed her eyes, shook her head, took several audible deep breaths, and pulled her lips into her mouth. I could tell this was not what she wanted to hear from me. She asked, "Well, why don't you introduce us to some of your contacts to help us make those connections? Isn't that also why we hired you?"

I channeled as much warmth and kindness in my body language and words as possible as I delivered information she wasn't going to like: "Because y'all ain't ready. Y'all aren't ready to meet my contacts. You would approach these communities the same way you always have, and your approach wouldn't connect. If I make that introduction and that happens, people I care about get hurt, and it's my reputation that takes a hit. I won't do that."

The dense, tense silence lingered between us for a few moments. "You don't know that," Marielle firmly pushed back.

The nerves in my body became extra tingly, an indicator that I needed to share more information that would be even harder for Marielle to absorb. "Marielle," I replied, "I *do* know that. My collaborators have told me they won't work with y'all because of your anti-Black and Brown approaches. They've also heard from their fellow community members that y'all aren't to be trusted." I braced myself for the response.

"What? Wait, what? That's our reputation?" Marielle questioned. Her armor diminished quickly, and she became very quiet as I watched disbelief wash over her. She heard the message.

I saw the opening to deepen our conversation and potentially build trust between us, so I offered, "I know that isn't what you wanted to hear, and I know that it sucks to hear it. You can help change that reputation."

Within a few months, Marielle made a complete turnaround. She never missed an equity or community engagement meeting again, she asked questions from a place of curiosity, and she read everything she could about racial justice and societal inequities. She also began attending community meetings led by local community members in the areas the organization aimed to reach. She listened. She built new relationships, deepened those with the people she supervised, and pushed the other leaders to improve their performance with their employees. She went from being someone her employees and communities avoided to being someone they saw as open, curious, willing to adapt, and caring. It took time.

One reason I prioritize working with individuals, especially in this way, is that too often I've seen antiracism conversations in organizations come to a halt the moment a leader or White employee becomes uncomfortable. Sadly, when White discomfort arrives, antiracism and DEI initiatives and programs are often either dissolved or relegated to performative gestures for a good PR moment.

In 2020 and 2021, an increasing number of people became interested in professionally engaging in antiracism and DEI work. These people were already subject matter experts in curriculum development, training, facilitation, marketing, leadership development, coaching, strategic planning, and a myriad of other areas. However, this work was different. In antiracism and equity work, you're often expected to be an expert in all areas, as well as to ensure the comfort of everyone, especially White people. The work is always multilayered. It centers the experiences and safety of those most harmed by racism and cultivates buy-in among those within institutional leadership and those with societal privileges. It includes educating organizations on racialized realities and present-day manifestations of historical racism.

And it guides everyone to see themselves in the work and as a part of the solution, equipping spaces with shared language, tools, and behavioral shifts to create more equitable environments.

A new individual coaching client came to me in 2021 with extensive facilitation and training experience. Amara had been in the wellness field for over twenty years and was excited to bring mindfulness, meditation, and yoga into her antiracism efforts. When I first met her, I asked about her personal antiracism goals and where she got stuck when engaging with others in the work. Initially she was unclear about her personal goals and was quick to share that she was frustrated by how often she felt like antiracism conversations inevitably came to a standstill. We paused to do a breathing exercise in that moment of stuckness.

"Why did you want to work with me?" I asked.

"Because you've been doing this for a long time, and I want to learn ways to push the work forward," she answered.

"Ah, I should clarify. I work with people who are unpacking their racism. I work with clients to reflect on and address racism in a supportive, accountable, and nonjudgmental manner; to reduce or eliminate bias in their decision-making, in life, and at work; to explore how racism has impacted their lives through benefits and harms, enabling them to live more authentically; to look inward. You are describing mentorship, consulting, or education."

I specified this because transforming into a racial justice champion requires examining our thoughts, narratives, mindsets, beliefs, and behaviors and aligning our unconscious minds with our conscious values, as we often ask others to do. There's often more power in being able to share your personal antiracism story and your relationship with racism than in focusing solely on external racism. Getting to the point where you can share your experience with racism requires curiosity, reflection, humility, intentionality, time, self-compassion, and commitment.

After a long pause and a lot of head nodding while looking at the floor, Amara looked up and said, "My personal goal ... is to let go of my sense of urgency and be present in the moment in antiracism conversations."

I smiled at her and asked, "Why is that an important goal for you?"

Tilting her head back and letting out a low, slow groan, she said, "Because when I operate from urgency, my anxiety takes over and I just want to get it done. I'm centering myself—my needs—and not the needs of the group."

Smiling again, I asked, "So, why is it important to you to be present in the moment in antiracism conversations?"

Amara smiled back, realizing my questions were supporting her in peeling back her layers. "A lot of reasons. I want my colleagues, especially my Black and Brown colleagues, to feel heard when they share their realities and truths. I want to honor their shares by following their lead. I want there to be space for dialogue, not just solutions. Also, I don't want anxiety to dictate how I show up in these spaces or in my life."

We continued to explore the messages in her mind that triggered her sense of urgency and anxiety. We examined the origin of these messages, verified their accuracy, and rewrote or reframed them from an empowered perspective. For example, we reexamined the message of, "I have to do a good job," which came with the message, "If I don't do a good job, then my colleagues won't trust me, my boss will get mad at me, or no one will want to work with me." I then asked Amara to describe what doing a good job looked like. She described feeling prepared, setting up the room a certain way, making sure the materials were in place, testing the technology, speaking with confidence, knowing all the answers to people's questions, interrupting resistant behaviors, having everyone engaged, and getting good feedback at the end from the participants and her cofacilitator. Essentially she described a good job as perfection with external validation.

I asked, "Tell me if I'm wrong, but what I got from what you shared is that you want to be exactly what each person needs to engage meaningfully in conversations about race and racism."

Amara smiled and shrugged her shoulders. "Well, yeah," she said. I then asked if she thought that was indeed possible, and she replied that it wasn't.

Next, I asked her whether she had asked her Black colleague with whom she'd been cofacilitating what his expectations of her were as the White facilitator in their cross-racial partnership. She told me they had met to divide up the tasks and determine who would lead each section in preparation for training. I repeated my question, and she told me she hadn't asked him about his expectations of her. When I asked whether they discussed what support and solidarity looked like as they cofacilitated, again the answer was no.

Amara began to laugh and placed her hands on her head, shaking it back and forth. "Ahh, I can't believe I didn't think to ask him those questions. I'd feel so much better knowing what he needs and wants from me in that space, I just never asked. I think if I felt aligned with him on navigating the day, I wouldn't feel so anxious. I wouldn't be overthinking everything."

By shifting her focus from making sure everyone felt comfortable and happy in the space to making sure her cofacilitator felt supported and she felt prepared, Amara reduced her anxiety and enabled herself to be more authentic, centered, and comfortable taking risks. To amplify her confidence and sense of presence, she began incorporating mindfulness and meditation into spaces where she facilitated antiracism conversations. She also incorporated antiracism into the yoga classes and meditation workshops she led as well as into her own mindfulness practices. As her work and practices intertwined, she felt more embodied in more spaces and put less pressure on herself to know everything and get everything right all the time.

For those of us who are White, that work begins within. It is be tempting to point outward—to the institutions, to the government, to our families—but first we must look inward. Excavating racism from our bodies, not just our minds, requires a willingness to sit in periods of discomfort. It also requires an understanding that White supremacy isn't just an external force; it was done to us and is embedded in the way we move through the world.[36] Undoing it will not happen overnight and might never be fully achieved, but we can choose, every day, to move toward something better.

I was raised on the promise of the American ideals of justice, freedom, and equality. I believed in the values written in our founding documents, the ones my teachers praised and my family upheld. Yet the older I grow, the more I realize that these ideals rarely manifested, especially for Black, Indigenous, and other People of Color. The values I was taught were not the values that shaped the world around me. This contradiction is painful but also clarifying. The work of antiracism is, at its core, about closing the gap between what we say we believe and what we actually practice. We must

---

36. Tema Okun, "(divorcing) White Supremacy Culture: Coming Home to Who We Really Are," White Supremacy Culture, accessed July 30, 2024, https://www.whitesupremacyculture.info/.

learn to appreciate the complexity of ourselves, the stories we absorb, and our histories. We must resist the urge to flatten narratives or assume that one voice speaks for all. No community is a monolith. And when Black, Indigenous, and other People of Color tell us their truths, we must believe them. Their experiences are not up for debate. Our role is to listen, learn, and act in solidarity.

We, as White people, must commit to unearthing the racism within us. We must challenge each other—our friends, our colleagues, our elected officials—when we see it perpetuated. We must recognize that racism is not a relic of the past but a powerful force that shapes our present. And if we genuinely believe in a future without racism, we must fight for it with intention, humility, and a willingness to be changed. Not everything will go as planned. Not everything will be comfortable. However, we do not do this work for our comfort. We do it because it's necessary. And we do not do it alone. The future is built in intersectional relationships with Black and Brown communities, with other minoritized communities, with leaders who've long been doing this work, with each other. The world we were taught to believe in is possible only if we commit to making it real. That is our responsibility. That is our work. And that is where we begin.

It's hard work, but isn't living up to our stated ideals worth it?

AFTERWORD

I've lived many lives and believe I still have many more to live. My journey has taken me across the country, gifting me with memories of people, places, and moments that have shaped who I am. I've always been drawn to water—beaches, lagoons, lakes—places where time dissolves into waves, reflection, and stillness. Water has been my teacher, offering both comfort and clarity.

My time in Seattle, where I met Casey, was full of lessons—some quiet, some jarring. I arrived as a Southern girl trying to make sense of a new, unfamiliar city. I was drawn to Puget Sound to reflect, to anchor myself, but I often left the beaches feeling unsettled. The water was cold, the sand coarse and sparse, the familiar treasures of a past life speckled with trips to Florida beaches—warm waves, soft shores, seashells—missing. I longed for what I knew.

Over time, though, the waters of the Sound began to teach me something deeper: My attachment to comfort and sameness ran beyond landscapes. I realized how often I sought what felt familiar, even in people and perspectives. I had to confront my own resistance to difference, to what challenged or unsettled me.

Casey's book reminds me of this process. With honesty and vulnerability, they invite us into the often-messy work of confronting bias, releasing comfort, and stepping into the unknown. Their words challenge us to see that the path to antiracism isn't neat or easy; it's deeply personal and often uncomfortable. But through that discomfort, something shifts. We begin to understand that the longing for belonging, connection, and humanity is universal.

These days, when I visit the beaches of the Pacific Northwest, I look for agates. At first glance they appear as plain gray stones, but when rinsed by a wave, they reveal layers of color, pattern, and beauty shaped by time and water. Much like this work of unlearning, opening, and transforming, agates remind me that what we first resist often holds the deepest potential for change.

Casey has shared something with the world that is beautifully brave and an invitation to the reader: Stay curious, stay open, and keep walking toward difference with the hope of finding something more whole on the other side.

Karimah Edwards

Founder and Principal Consultant at Humming Voices

ACKNOWLEDGMENTS

No matter how much I learn, how deeply I engage, or how many interracial relationships I hold in my life, my racial privilege is always present. My presence as a White person can create a threat in multiracial spaces whether I intend it to or not. That's part of the reality of Whiteness in this country.

I will never know what it's like to live in a Black or Brown body in the US, nor will I ever know the weight of what it's like to carry racialized intergenerational trauma. It's not only untrue but also profoundly disrespectful to suggest that the oppressions I face in other aspects of my identity are the same. They are not. I recognize the crucial difference between bias, discrimination, and racism. As someone who's queer, nonbinary, disabled, and middle-aged, I've experienced bias and discrimination, but I only benefit from racism. And it's precisely because of that truth that I'm committed to continuing the work of unlearning, accountability, and action.

This book, like my life's work, is the result of the generosity, brilliance, and trust of so many people who've taught me, challenged me, and walked with me on this imperfect journey. I'm sincerely and humbly grateful to those who've supported my continuous learning, unlearning, and engagement with antiracism, including but not limited to Darlene Flynn, Kyana Wheeler, Natalie Hunter, Felicia Caldwell, Brenda Anibarro, Marcella Wilson, Mary Mitchell, Karimah Edwards, Glenn Harris, Catrina Cuevas, Dr. Andrea Ramirez, Lauren Kite, Barb Graff, and countless others whose names and labor have left indelible marks on my growth.

Thank you to my clients and colleagues who've entrusted me to walk beside them in this work. Your courage, vulnerability, and commitment inspire me daily.

A huge shout-out to Jenn T. Grace and Publish Your Purpose's Getting Started for Authors Program. Thank you to my fellow participants, Julia Bowan, Cathy Alfandre, Natalie Suppes, Connie Perkins-Allaire, and Chris Agnos; I had no idea of the work it would take to write this book, and without you I wouldn't have seen it through to completion.

A special thank you to Dara Joyce Lurie for her immense coaching and support in digging deeper every step of the way, and to Nancy Graham-Tillman for stepping in at a moment when I felt as though this book would never get done. You helped get this book to the next level.

I'm immensely grateful to Peggy McIntosh, author of the article "White Privilege: Unpacking the Invisible Knapsack," and to Nancy Rust Myers, author of the article "The 5 Stages of White Privilege Awareness." Their work helped me reflect more deeply and consequentially, and I was humbled by their words of wisdom and encouragement as I wrote this book.

And to my beloved Jennifer Wong, no words could fully hold the depth of my gratitude for you. You are beyond what I ever believed I deserved. Loving you and being loved by you is the greatest gift of my life. May I continue to earn the gift of your love until the end of my days.

This book is not a destination. It's a reflection of an ongoing process, one shaped by community, truth-telling, and love. Thank you for being part of it.

APPENDIX A

Glossary of Terms

These definitions are adapted from and are a compilation of those from *Merriam Webster's Collegiate Dictionary*, Ibram X. Kendi's *How to Be an Antiracist*, the Center for the Study of Social Policy, *Psychology Today*, the US Conference of Catholic Bishops, the Anti-Oppression Network, and Racial Equity Tools.

accountability: In the context of racial equity work, accountability refers to the ways in which individuals and communities hold themselves to their goals and actions and acknowledge the values and groups to which they are responsible.

antiracism: The active process of identifying and challenging racism by changing systems, organizational structures, policies, practices, and attitudes to redistribute power in an equitable manner.

antiracist: Someone who supports an antiracist policy through their actions or by expressing antiracist ideas. This includes the expression of ideas that racial groups are equals and do not need developing and supporting policies that reduce **racial inequity**.

awareness: The ability to judge a situation accurately from one's own viewpoint and the viewpoints of members in other cultures, including the historical context of oppression and current sociopolitical awareness when judging such situations. It is being able to identify and interpret the multiple layers of one's own and others' social identities, social group statuses, power, privileges, oppression, strengths, limitations, assumptions, attitudes, values, beliefs, and biases. Awareness recognizes culturally learned assumptions of one's own and other cultures' races, genders, classes, sexual orientations, abilities, religions, education levels, physical sizes, and national origins.

baptism: The initial Sacrament of Initiation of the Catholic Church, baptism is a ritual in which one, often an infant, is blessed and/or bathed in holy water by a priest. This ritual serves to welcome the person into the church and as a child of God. It is also a ritual to prevent the person, often an infant, from going to purgatory or hell in case of their death.

bias: A tendency, inclination, or prejudice toward or against something or someone. Biases are often based on stereotypes rather than actual knowledge of an individual or circumstance, and such cognitive shortcuts can result in prejudgments that lead to rash decisions or discriminatory practices.

BIPOC: A term referring to "Black and/or Indigenous People of Color." While just "POC" or "People of Color" is often used as well, BIPOC explicitly leads with Black and Indigenous identities, which helps to counter anti-Black racism and invisibilization of Native communities.

Catholic: A member of the Catholic Church.

Catholicism: The traditions and beliefs of the Catholic Church, often referring to its theology, liturgy, morals, rituals, and practices.

caucus: An intentionally created space for those who share an identity to convene for learning, support, and connections. Caucuses based on racial identity are often respectfully composed of People of Color, White people, people who hold multiracial identities, or people who share specific racial or ethnic identities.

cisgender (pronounced *sis-gender*): Used to refer to an individual whose gender identity aligns with the sex assigned to them at birth. The prefix *cis-* comes from the Latin word for "on the same side as." People who are both cisgender and heterosexual are sometimes referred to as "cishet" (pronounced *sis-het*) individuals. The term is not a slur, and people who are not trans should avoid calling themselves "normal" and instead refer to themselves as cisgender or cis.

classism: A system of oppression that produces social and physical barriers based on one's real or perceived economic status or background. It is associated with but not mutually exclusive to capitalism. While we may describe classes as "poor," "low income," "working class," "middle class," and "upper class," a binary also exists within classism. This binary exploits poor, low-income, and working-class people for the benefit of middle- and upper-class individuals.

colorblindness: Also known as "colorblind ideology" or "color evasiveness," colorblindness in racial contexts purports to not noticing race in an effort to not appear racist. It asserts that ending discrimination merely requires treating individuals as equally as possible, without regard to race, culture, or ethnicity. By overlooking the cumulative and enduring ways in which race unequally shapes life chances and opportunities for people from different groups, colorblindness actually reinforces and sustains an unequal status quo. By leaving structural inequalities in place, colorblindness has become the "new racism." It also ignores cultural attributes that people value and deserve to have recognized and affirmed.

Communion (Eucharist): A demonstration of unity with God, performed by his people and with prayer for the Holy Spirit to bring unity under God for all of humanity by ingesting the body and blood of life (wafers and wine).

Confirmation: Makes a person more complete in the image of God so that they may bear witness to Him before the world and work to bring the Body of Christ to its fullness.

Confraternity of Christian Doctrine (CCD): Early education lessons on Christian and Catholic teachings.

cultural humility: A concept coined and developed by Dr. Melanie Tervalon and Dr. Jann Murray-Garcia, rooted in their experiences as practitioners in the medical field in the 1990s. As a practice, it stresses a commitment to lifelong learning and self-critique that aims to correct power imbalances inherent in structured, institutionalized relationships. Cultural humility can also be practiced by individuals with societal privileges when engaging interpersonally with someone without those same privileges.

cultural racism: The representations, messages, and stories conveying the idea that behaviors and values associated with White people or "Whiteness" are automatically "better" or more "normal" than those associated with other racially defined groups. Cultural racism shows up in advertising, movies, history books, definitions of patriotism, and policies and laws. Cultural racism is also a powerful force in maintaining systems of internalized supremacy and internalized racism because it influences collective beliefs about what constitutes appropriate behavior, what is seen as beautiful, and the value placed on various forms of expression. All these cultural norms and values in the US have explicitly or implicitly racialized ideals and assumptions (e.g., what "nude" means as a color, which facial features and body types are considered beautiful, and which child-rearing practices are considered appropriate).

culture: A social system of meanings and customs developed by a group of people to assure their adaptation and survival. These groups are distinguished by a set of unspoken rules that shape values, beliefs, habits, patterns of thinking, behaviors, and styles of communication.

discrimination: The unequal treatment of members of various groups based on race, gender, social class, sexual orientation, physical ability, religion, or other categories.

diversity: Includes all the ways in which people differ and encompasses all the different characteristics that make one individual or group different from another. It is all-inclusive and recognizes everyone and every group as part of the diversity that should be valued. A broad definition includes not only race, ethnicity, and gender—the groups that most often come to mind when the term is used—but also age, national origin, religion, disability, sexual orientation, socioeconomic status, education, marital status, language, and physical appearance. It also involves different ideas, perspectives, and values.

equity: When everyone is treated fairly. An emphasis on equity seeks to render justice by deeply considering structural factors that benefit some social groups or communities and harm other social groups or communities. Sometimes justice demands, for the purpose of equity, an unequal response.

ethnicity: A social construct that divides people into smaller social groups based on characteristics such as a shared sense of group membership, values, behavioral patterns, language, political and economic interests, histories, and ancestral geographical bases.

ethnocentrism: Judging another culture solely by the values and standards of one's own culture; the view of things in which one's own group is the center of everything and all others are scaled and rated with reference to it. An ethnocentric individual judges other groups relative to their own, especially with concern to language, behavior, customs, and religion.

gender: Broadly, a set of socially constructed roles, behaviors, activities, and attributes that a given society considers appropriate.

gender identity: One's deeply held core sense of self in relation to gender. Gender identity does not always correspond to biological sex; people become aware of their gender identity at many different stages of life, from as early as eighteen months and into adulthood. Gender identity is a separate concept from sexuality and gender expression.

heterosexism: Structural, interpersonal, or other forms of discrimination or prejudice against anyone who does not conform to binary gender norms based on the assumption that heterosexuality is the normal or correct sexual orientation.

implicit biases: Also known as "unconscious" or "hidden" biases, implicit biases are negative associations that people unknowingly hold; they are expressed automatically, without conscious awareness. Many studies have indicated that implicit biases affect an individual's attitudes and actions, thus creating real-world implications even though individuals may not even be aware that those biases exist within themselves. Notably, implicit biases have been shown to trump an individual's stated commitments to equality and fairness, thereby producing behavior that diverges from the explicit attitudes that many people profess. The Implicit Association Test is often used to measure implicit biases with regard to race, gender, sexual orientation, age, religion, and other topics.

inclusion: Authentically bringing traditionally excluded individuals and/or groups into processes, activities, decisions, and policy making in a way that shares power.

individual racism: The beliefs, attitudes, and actions of individuals that support or perpetuate racism. Individual racism can be deliberate, or individuals may act to perpetuate or support racism without knowing that is what they are doing.

institutional racism: Refers specifically to the ways in which institutional policies and practices create different outcomes for different racial groups. The institutional policies may never mention any racial group, but their effect is to create advantages for Whites and oppression and disadvantage for people from groups classified as People of Color.

internalized racism: The situation that occurs in a racist system when a racial group oppressed by racism supports the supremacy and dominance of the dominating group by maintaining or participating in the set of attitudes, behaviors, social structures, and ideologies that undergird the dominating group's power. It involves four essential and interconnected elements:

1. *Decision-making*: Due to racism, People of Color do not have the ultimate decision-making power over the decisions that control their lives and resources. As a result, on a personal level they may think White people know more about what needs to be done than they do. On an interpersonal level, they may not support each other's authority and power, especially if it is in opposition to the dominating racial group. Structurally, there is a system in place that rewards People of Color who support White supremacy and power and coerces or punishes those who do not.

2. *Resources*: Broadly defined (e.g., money, time, etc.), resources are unequally in the hands and under the control of White people. Internalized racism is the system in place that makes it difficult for People of Color to get access to and control the resources for their own communities. One learns to believe that serving and using resources for themselves and their particular communities is not serving "everybody."

3. *Standards*: With internalized racism, the standards that People of Color accept as appropriate or "normal" are White people's or Eurocentric standards. One has difficulty naming, communicating, and living up to their deepest standards and values and holding themselves and others accountable to them.

4. *Naming the problem*: There is a system in place that misnames the problem of racism as a problem of is or caused by People of Color and blames the dis-ease—emotional, economic, political, or otherwise—on People of Color. With internalized racism, People of Color might, for example, believe they are more violent than White people and not consider state-sanctioned political violence or the hidden or privatized violence of White people and the systems they put in place and support.

interpersonal racism: Racism that occurs between individuals. When one brings their private beliefs into their interactions with others, racism lands in the interpersonal realm.

Islamophobia: A form of religious bigotry with strong racial components that scapegoats and demonizes Muslims and those perceived to be Muslim. Since the war on terror era, Islamophobia has intensified as a central narrative and policy agenda for the Right in the US and Europe, and it often dovetails with anti-immigrant xenophobia, Christian nationalism, and a broader conspiratorial worldview. Islamophobia frequently leads to Islamophobic violence, and it can be structural, institutional, interpersonal, and/or internalized. Note that although the term is in common usage, the *-phobia* suffix suggests individual bigotry to the exclusion of systemic and structural forces, so the form "anti-Muslim" is generally preferred.

meritocracy: a system, organization, or society in which people are chosen and moved into positions of success, power, and influence on the basis of their demonstrated abilities and merit.

microaggression: The everyday verbal, nonverbal, and environmental slights, snubs, or insults, whether intentional or unintentional, that communicate hostile, derogatory, or negative messages to target persons based solely upon their marginalized group membership.

minoritized: A social process by which individuals or groups are intentionally or unintentionally distanced from access to power and resources and constructed as insignificant, peripheral, or less valuable or privileged to a community or "mainstream" society. The term describes a social process so as not to imply a lack of agency. Minoritized groups or people are those excluded from mainstream social, economic, cultural, or political life.

misogyny: An aggravated form of sexism. Misogyny is a primary motivation for the Right, both as a vehicle for recruitment and as justification for its agenda, that seeks to maintain traditional gender roles, limit reproductive and bodily autonomy, and situate marginalized genders as lesser than male.

mortal sin(s): An act that breaks off one's relationship with God; it is the equivalent of spiritual death.

nonbinary: People who do not subscribe to the gender binary; they might exist between or beyond the man–woman binary. Some use the term exclusively, while others may use it interchangeably with terms such as "genderqueer," "gender fluid," "gender nonconforming," "gender diverse," or "gender expansive."

oppression: The systematic subjugation of one social group by a more powerful social group for the social, economic, and political benefit of the more powerful social group. Per Racial Equity Tools, Rita Hardiman and Bailey Jackson state that oppression exists when the following four conditions are found:

1. The oppressor group has the power to define reality for themselves and others.
2. The target groups take in and internalize the negative messages about themselves and end up

cooperating with the oppressors (thinking and acting like them).

3. Genocide, harassment, and discrimination are systematic and institutionalized so that individuals are not necessary to keep it going.

4. Members of both the oppressor and target groups are socialized to play their roles as normal and correct.

Oppression = Power + Prejudice

patriarchy: A historically based, institutionally perpetuated system of exploitation and oppression in which those assigned male or those exhibiting characteristics that have been assigned male hold ultimate authority and privilege central to social organization, occupying roles of political leadership, moral authority, and control of property. It implies and entails female subordination and can result in gendered outcomes even without specific gendered animus articulated between individuals.

Penance (Confession): The act of asking for forgiveness from God and being pardoned by Him through a priest.

power: Unequally distributed globally and in US society, some individuals or groups wield greater power than others, thereby allowing them greater access and control over resources. Wealth, Whiteness, citizenship, patriarchy, heterosexism, and education are a few key social mechanisms through which power operates. Although the term is often conceptualized as power over other individuals or groups, other variations are "power with" (used in the context of building collective strength) and "power within" (referring to one's internal strength). Learning to "see" and understand relations of power is vital to organizing for progressive social change.

prejudice: A prejudgment, or unjustifiable, and usually negative attitude of one type of individual or group toward another group and its members. Such negative attitudes are typically based on unsupported general-izations or stereotypes that deny the right of individual members of certain groups to be recognized and treated as individuals with individual characteristics.

privilege: Unearned social power accorded by the formal and informal institutions of society to *all* members of a dominant group (e.g., White privilege, male privilege, etc.). Privilege is usually invisible to those who have it because they are taught not to see it, but it nevertheless puts them at an advantage over those who do not have it.

race: For many people, it comes as a surprise that racial categorization schemes were invented by scientists to support worldviews that some groups of people are superior and some are inferior. There are three important concepts linked to this fact:

1. Race is a made-up social construct, not an actual biological fact.
2. Race designations have changed over time; some groups that are considered "White" in the US today were considered "non-White" in previous eras, whether in US Census data or in mass media and popular culture (e.g., Irish, Italian, and Jewish people).
3. The way in which racial categorizations are enforced (the shape of racism) has also changed over time. For example, the racial designation of Asian American and Pacific Islander changed four times in the nineteenth century, meaning at times they were defined as White and at other times as not White. As designated groups, Asian Americans and Pacific Islanders have been used by Whites at different times in history to compete with African American labor.

racial equity: The condition that would be achieved if one's racial identity no longer predicted in a statistical sense how they fare. When using the term, most people are usually thinking about racial equity only as one part of racial justice, thus society needs to work to address the root causes of inequities, not just their manifestations. This includes elimination of policies, practices, attitudes, and cultural messages that reinforce differential outcomes by race or that fail to eliminate them.

racial inequity: When two or more racial groups are not standing on approximately equal footing, such as the percentages of each ethnic group in terms of dropout rates, single-family home ownership, and access to healthcare.

racial justice: The systematic fair treatment of people of all races that results in equitable opportunities and outcomes for all. Racial justice, or racial equity, goes beyond "antiracism" in that it is not just the absence of discrimination and inequities but also the presence of deliberate systems and supports to achieve and sustain racial equity through proactive and preventive measures.

racialization: The very complex and contradictory process through which groups come to be designated as being of a particular "race" and on that basis subjected to differential and/or unequal treatment. Per Racial Equity Tools, "Put simply, 'racialization [is] the process of manufacturing and utilizing the notion of race in any capacity.'" While White people are also racialized, this process is often rendered invisible or normative to those designated as White. As a result, White people may not see themselves as part of a race but still maintain the authority to name and racialize "others."

racism: Different from racial prejudice, hatred, or discrimination, racism involves one group having the power to carry out systematic discrimination through the institutional policies and practices of a society and by shaping the cultural beliefs and values that support those racist policies and practices.

> Racism = race prejudice + social and institutional power
> Racism = a system of advantage based on race
> Racism = a system of oppression based on race
> Racism = a White supremacy system

racist: One who supports a racist policy through their actions or interactions or by expressing a racist idea.

Sacraments of Initiation: Rituals and practices by which faith is expressed and strengthened between one and God and the Church, supporting one's sanctification.

sexism: A system that produces social and physical barriers based on gender, specifically for girls and women. Sexism historically conflates one's sex (genitalia, anatomy, chromosomes, hormones, and reproductive organs) with gender (expression and identity) and depends on the gender binary of women and men.

sexual orientation: The sexual attraction toward other people or no people. While sexual activity involves the choices one makes regarding behavior, one's sexual activity does not define one's sexual orientation. Sexual orientation is part of the human condition, and all people have one. Typically, it is attraction that helps determine orientation.

social oppression: Oppression that is achieved through social means and is social in scope, meaning it affects whole categories of people. This kind of oppression includes the systematic mistreatment, exploitation, and abuse of a group (or groups) of people by another group (or groups). It occurs whenever one group holds power over another in society through the control of social institutions along with society's laws, customs, and norms. The outcome of social oppression is that groups in society are sorted into different positions within the social hierarchies of race, class, gender, sexuality, and ability. Those in the controlling, or dominant, group benefit from the oppression of other groups through heightened privileges relative to others, greater access to rights and resources, better quality of life, and overall greater life chances. Those who experience the brunt of oppression have fewer rights, less access to resources, less political power, lower economic potential, worse health and higher mortality rates, and lower overall life chances.

socialization: The process of consciously and unconsciously learning norms, beliefs, and practices from individuals, media, and institutions about who does and does not have power and privilege as it relates to social identities and how the self is positioned in relationship to these identities. In other words, it determines how one is "supposed" to act.

structural racism: Also known as "systemic racism," structural racism is the normalization and legitimization of an array of dynamics—historical, cultural, institutional, and interpersonal—that routinely advantage White people while producing cumulative and chronic adverse outcomes for People of Color. This type of racism encompasses the entire system of White domination and is diffused and infused into all aspects of society, including its history, culture, politics, economics, and entire social fabric. Structural racism is more difficult to locate in a particular institution because it involves the reinforcing effects of multiple institutions and cultural norms, past and present, which continually reproduces old forms of racism and produces new ones. Structural racism is the most profound and pervasive form of racism; all other forms emerge from structural racism.

transgender: Often shortened to "trans" from the Latin prefix for "on a different side as," this term describes one's gender identity that does not necessarily match their assigned sex at birth. Transgender people may or may not decide to alter their bodies hormonally and/or surgically to match their gender identity. This word is also used as an umbrella term to describe groups of people who transcend conventional expectations of gender identity or expression, such as but not limited to people who identify as transsexual, genderqueer, gender variant, gender diverse, and androgynous. The shortened version is often considered more inclusive because it includes transgender, transsexual, transmasc, transfem, and those who simply use the word trans.

venial sin(s): A less serious sin in which the relationship between one and God is not broken. However, venial sins make one open to temptation and more susceptible to committing a mortal sin.

White fragility: A state in which even a minimum amount of racial stress becomes intolerable (for White people) and triggers a range of defensive moves. These moves include the outward display of emotions such as anger, fear, and guilt, as well as behaviors such as argumentation, silence, and leaving the stress-inducing situation. In turn, these behaviors function to reinstate White racial equilibrium.

White privilege: The unquestioned and unearned set of advantages, entitlements, benefits, and choices bestowed on people solely because they are White. Generally, White people who experience such privilege do so without being conscious of it.

White supremacy: The idea (ideology) that White people and the ideas, thoughts, beliefs, and actions of White people are superior to the ideas, thoughts, beliefs, and actions of People of Color. While most people associate White supremacy with extremist groups such as the Ku Klux Klan and the neo-Nazis, White supremacy is ever present in our institutional and cultural assumptions that assign value, morality, goodness, and humanity to the White group while casting people and Communities of Color as worthless (worth less), immoral, bad, inhuman, or undeserving. Drawing from critical race theory, the term also refers to a political or socioeconomic system in which White people enjoy structural advantage and rights that other racial and ethnic groups do not, both at a collective and an individual level.

White Supremacy Culture: The dominant, unquestioned standards of behavior and ways of functioning embodied by the vast majority of institutions in the US. These standards may be seen as mainstream, dominant cultural practices and have evolved from the US's history of White supremacy. Because it is so normalized, it can be hard to see, which only adds to its powerful hold.

In many ways, it is indistinguishable from what one might call US culture or norms—a focus on individuals over groups, for example, or an emphasis on the written word as a form of professional communication—but it operates in even more subtle ways by actually defining what "normal" is and, likewise, what "professional," "effective," or even "good" is. In turn, White culture also defines what is not good, what is "at risk," and what is "unsustainable." White culture values some ways of thinking, behaving, deciding, and knowing—ways that are more familiar and come more naturally to those from a White, Western tradition—while devaluing or rendering other ways invisible. And it does this without ever having to explicitly say so.

Whiteness: Using the term "White" when referring to people was initiated by Virginia slave owners and colonial rulers in the seventeenth century. It replaced terms such as "Christian" and "Englishman" to distinguish European colonists from Africans and Indigenous peoples. European colonial powers established Whiteness as a legal concept after Bacon's Rebellion in 1676, during which indentured servants of European and African descent united against the colonial elite. The legal distinction of White separated the servant class on the basis of skin color and continental origin, so the creation of

"Whiteness" meant giving privileges to some while denying them to others, with the justification of biological and social inferiority. Whiteness itself refers to the specific dimensions of racism that serve to elevate White people over People of Color.

APPENDIX B

*1980–1999 Extended Timeline of Some
Major US and Global Events*

Extended

- Nuclear arms race and protests (1942–1987)
- Cold War (1945–1991)
- South African Apartheid (1948–1993)
- Vietnam War (1955–1975)
- Eritrea's War for Independence from Ethiopian rule (1961–1993)
- Nicaraguan Revolution (1960s–1990)
- Northern Ireland Conflict (1968–1998)
- Lebanese Civil War (1975–1990)
- Operation Litani: Israel invades Lebanon (1978–1982)
- Angolan Civil War (1975–2002)
- Iran Hostage Crisis (1979–1981)
- Soviet–Afghan War (1979–1989)
- Iran–Iraq War (1980–1988)

- South Lebanon War and South Lebanon Conflict (1982–2000)
- First Intifada (Palestinian uprising against Israel in Gaza and West Bank) (1987–1993)
- Second Intifada (Palestinian uprising against Israel in Gaza and West Bank) (2000–2005)

1980

- The Gwangju Massacre in South Korea occurs.
- China's population reaches one billion; China creates the One Child Policy.
- Zimbabwe gains independence from Britain.
- Cuban Haitian Entrant Program (CHEP) is established.
- Liberian Coup takes place.
- Miami Riots occurs following the acquittal of White police officers in the brutal beating and killing of Arthur McDuffie, a Black man, during a traffic stop.

1981

- Global recession (1981–1982).
- MTV launches.
- US Senate bombed by left-wing group Weather Underground, protesting US foreign policies.
- Pope John Paul II is shot in an attempted assassination.
- CDC publishes its first official report on GRID, later known as the AIDS virus.

- Egyptian President Anwar Sadat is assassinated.
- Sandra Day O'Conner becomes first White female Supreme Justice.
- Royal wedding of Princess Diana and Prince Charles.
- Assassination attempt of Ronald Reagan.

1982

- *USA Today* becomes the first nationwide newspaper.
- The Commodore 64 personal computer is unveiled at the Consumer Electronics show in Las Vegas.
- Michael Jackson releases his best-selling album *Thriller*.
- Vincent Chin, a Chinese American man, is brutally beaten to death by two White autoworkers who blamed Asian Americans for the decline of the US auto industry; despite the murder being racially motivated, the perpetrators receive no jail time, sparking nationwide protests and mobilizing the modern Asian American Civil Rights Movement.
- The Falklands War takes place.
- Three abortion clinics are bombed in Washington, DC, in a coordinated right-wing attack.
- The Supreme Court in *Nixon v. Fitzgerald* establishes presidential immunity from civil damages liability arising from official acts performed in office.

1983

- Sally Ride becomes the first White female astronaut.
- Reagan calls the Soviet Union an "evil empire."
- The movie *The Day After* airs across the US.
- Mount Kilauea begins the Pu'u 'Ō'ō eruption (1983), which continues until 2018.
- Darryl Gates, a Black man, is severely beaten by LAPD officers during a traffic stop, highlighting growing racial tensions between Black communities and police in Los Angeles.
- Military barracks in Beirut are attacked by Hezbollah, killing 299 people.
- US invades Granada.
- Left-wing group Armed Resistance Unit bombs the US Senate, protesting US foreign policies.
- Drought and war cause Eritrean–Ethiopia Famine, killing and displacing millions.
- The Soviet Union shoots down Korea Air Lines Flight 007, killing all 269 people on board.
- The US Embassy is bombed in Kuwait by Hezbollah, killing five people.
- Ronald Reagan signs legislation making MLK Jr. Day an official federal holiday.
- Ronald Reagan launches the Strategic Defensive Initiative, a.k.a. Star Wars.

1984

- AT&T, a.k.a. Bell System, is broken up into regional phone companies, breaking up its prior monopoly.
- *The Cosby Show* premiers.
- Bruce Springsteen releases "Born in the USA."
- Eleanor Bumpurs, a sixty-six-year-old Black woman, is shot and killed by NYPD officers during an eviction, becoming a symbol of excessive force against Black citizens.
- Indira Gandhi, India's prime minister, is assassinated.
- Charles Howard, a gay man, is attacked, thrown off a bridge, and murdered in Maine by three teenagers.
- Firebombing attack at the Feminist Women's Health Center in Florida.
- Radio host Alan Berg is assassinated by right-wing White supremacist group The Order in Colorado for speaking out against anti-Semitism and White supremacy.

1985

- Mikhail Gorbachev replaces Leonid Brezhnev as the leader of the Soviet Union.
- TWA Flight 847 is hijacked, with one killed and hostages held for sixteen days.
- Air India Flight 182 is bombed by the Canadian Khalistan Movement, killing all 329 people on board.

- Philadelphia Police Department bombs a Black separatist group location, MOVE, killing eleven people and destroying sixty-one homes.
- White supremacist Patrick Purdy opens fire at Cleveland Elementary School in California, killing five children and injuring thirty-two others.
- "We Are the World" is recorded by more than forty-five American singers and raises seventy-five million dollars to feed people in Africa facing starvation.
- Nintendo Entertainment System is released in the US.

1986

- MLK Day becomes an official federal holiday.
- Space shuttle *Challenger* explodes with teacher Christa McAuliffe on board.
- The Iran–Contra Affair is exposed.
- The Soviet Union launches the Mir Space Station, preceding the International Space Station.
- The People Power Revolution ousts Philippines Prime Minister Ferdinand Marco.
- Swedish Prime Minister Olof Palme is assassinated.
- Microsoft goes public on the New York Stock Exchange.
- Hands Across America attempts to form a human chain from New York to California to raise money to fight hunger and homelessness.

- Scientists on a Cold War mission discover the wreckage of the Titanic.
- An Idaho-based White supremacist group commits an arson attack on Temple Beth Shalom in Washington State.
- The explosion at the Chernobyl Nuclear Power Plant scatters radioactive materials across Europe.
- White Christian nationalists bomb five abortion clinics in Florida, Georgia, and Tennessee.
- *The Oprah Winfrey Show* airs nationally

1987

- Terry Waite, a special envoy for the Anglican Church, is kidnapped in Beirut and held until 1991.
- Burkina Faso President Thomas Sankara is assassinated.
- The trial of Nikolaus "Klaus" Barbie, the Nazi "Butcher of Lyon," begins in France.
- Ronald Reagan visits West Berlin and challenges Mikhail Gorbachev to "tear down this wall," referring to the Berlin Wall erected in 1961 as a part of the Cold War.
- A gunman takes forty-one people hostage at a Korean American-owned electronics store in California, ranting about his hatred for Asian immigrants.
- Taiwan ends thirty-eight years of martial law.
- Former Nazi Rudolf Hess commits suicide in a German prison.

- Margaret Thatcher wins third term as Prime Minister of the UK.

1988

- The USS Vincennes shoots down the passenger plane Iran Airlines Flight 655, mistaking it for a F-14 Tomcat and killing all 290 aboard.
- Osama bin Laden forms Al Qaeda.
- Al Qaeda assassinates Afghan Taliban resistance leader Ahmad Shah Massoud.
- The Iran–Iraq war ends with an estimated death toll of more than one million people.
- First annual AIDS Day is held.
- Mulugeta Seraw, an Ethiopian immigrant, is beaten to death by White supremacists in Oregon.
- White supremacist Richard Lee Snell opens fire at a gay bar in Pennsylvania, injuring several patrons.
- Pan Am Flight 103 explodes in Lockerbie, Scotland, killing 259 on board and eleven people on the ground; a Libyan intelligence officer is convicted of the attack.

1989

- Japanese Emperor Hirohito dies, ending a sixty-two-year reign.
- The Exxon Valdez Oil Spill taints hundreds of miles of Alaskan coastline.

- Students march through Beijing to Tiananmen Square, calling for a more democratic government; after a few months of peaceful and increasing protests, Chinese troops fire on civilians, killing an unknown number of people in the Tiananmen Square Massacre.
- General Colin Powell becomes the first Black male to be appointed to head the Joint Chiefs of Staff.
- Yvonne Smallwood, a Black man, is shot and killed by NYPD officers under controversial circumstances, sparking community outrage.
- An arson attack occurs on Upstairs Lounge, a memorial honoring the thirty-two patrons killed and fifteen patrons injured during the 1973 Upstairs Lounge Fire.
- The Berlin Wall falls.
- US troops invade Panama.
- Leonard Kravitz is stabbed in New York by a group of White supremacist skinheads.
- An arson attack destroys an abortion clinic in Virginia.
- A White supremacist opens fire at Cleveland Elementary School in California, killing five Southeast Asian children and wounding thirty-two others.
- The Central Park Five (later known as the Exonerated Five), five Black and Latino teenagers falsely accused of rape and vilified with racist rhetoric in the media, are arrested, sparking Central Park Protests.

1990

- Global recession (1990–1991).
- A White supremacist group carries out multiple bank robberies in the Midwest to fund their extremist activities (throughout the 1990s).
- A White supremacist group engages in multiple shootings and assaults throughout the country (throughout the 1990s).
- The first McDonald's opens in Moscow, Russia.
- Lebanese Prime Minister Rashid Karami is assassinated.
- Paul Broussard, a gay man, is attacked and murdered by a group of teenagers in Texas.
- Iraq invades Kuwait, leading to the Gulf War.
- Germany is reunified after the fall of the Berlin Wall.

1991

- The Gulf War (Operation Desert Storm) begins as a US-led coalition attacks Iraq.
- The Soviet Union collapses, marking the end of the Cold War.
- LAPD officers brutally beat Rodney King after a high-speed chase; the assault is caught on camera and sparks national outrage.
- The former Indian Prime Minister is assassinated.
- A Jewish driver accidentally strikes two seven-year-old children of Guyanese immigrants, killing one and

severely injuring the other and sparking the Crown Heights Riots, clashes between Black and Jewish residents; Yankel Rosenbaum, an Australian Jewish man, is attacked and killed during the riots.

1992

- The US and Russia sign the START II treaty, reducing nuclear weapons.
- Bill Clinton is elected as the forty-second US president.
- An arson attack occurs at Eagles Wing, a lesbian bar in Oregon.
- Los Angeles riots follow the acquittal of police officers in the Rodney King beating case, resulting in sixty-three deaths and over two thousand injuries.

1993

- Bill Clinton is inaugurated as US president.
- The World Trade Center bombing occurs in New York City.
- Dr. David Gunn, an abortion care provider, is assassinated in Florida.
- The Waco Siege ends in a deadly fire after a standoff between the FBI and the Branch Davidians.
- An attempted shooting occurs at North Valley Jewish Community Center in California by a White supremacist.

- Brandon Teena, a transgender man, is raped and murdered by homophobic men in Nebraska.
- South African Anti-Apartheid Leader Chris Hani is assassinated in an attempt to derail South Africa's transition to democracy.
- Dr. George Tiller, an abortion care provider, is shot five times in Kansas; he survives the attack.

1994

- Rwandan President Juvenal Habyarimana and Burundi President Cyprien Ntaryamira are assassinated, sparking the Rwandan Genocide.
- The Rwandan Genocide begins, leading to the deaths of nearly eight hundred thousand people.
- Israel and the Palestine Liberation Organization sign the Oslo Accords.
- Dr. John Britton, an abortion provider, and James Barrett, his security escort, are assassinated outside a clinic in Florida.
- Nicholas Heyward Jr., a thirteen-year-old Black boy, is shot and killed by NYPD officer Brian George while playing with a toy gun in a stairwell; the officer is not charged.
- OJ Simpson is arrested for murder after a highway chase caught on camera.
- Republicans win control of both chambers of Congress for the first time in forty years.

- Shannon Lowney and Leanne Nichols, abortion clinic workers, are assassinated while working at the front desk of their clinics.

1995

- The Oklahoma City bombing, a domestic terrorist attack committed by anti-government White supremacists, kills 168 people and injures more than six hundred.
- The Srebrenica Massacre occurs during the Bosnian War.
- Israeli Prime Minister Yitzhak Rabin is assassinated.
- A firebombing destroys a Planned Parenthood in Washington State.
- Hundreds of thousands of Black men march in Washington DC, calling for racial justice, unity, and personal responsibility in the Million Man March organized by Louis Farrakhan and the Nation of Islam.
- Thien Minh Ly, a Vietnamese American college student, is stabbed to death by a White supremacist while rollerblading in California.
- OJ Simpson is acquitted of murder; reactions split across racial lines.
- White supremacist individuals and groups bomb more than thirty Black churches between 1995 and 1996 in Tennessee, South Carolina, Georgia, North Carolina, Louisiana, Oklahoma, Virginia, Texas, Florida, Mississippi, Oregon, and Alabama, sparking national protests.

1996

- The Atlanta Olympic Park bombing occurs.
- Prince Charles and Princess Diana divorce.
- Bill Clinton is reelected as US president.
- White supremacists kill the Mueller family in Ohio.
- White supremacists plan to bomb a Martin Luther King Jr. parade in Washington State but are arrested before the attack.
- Bombings occur at two abortion clinics in Georgia; the bomber is later linked to the Olympic Park bombing.

1997

- The first *Harry Potter* book is published.
- Great Britain agrees to hand control of Hong Kong over to China.
- Abner Louima, a Haitian immigrant, is brutally beaten and sexually assaulted with a broomstick by NYPD officers in a Brooklyn precinct; Officer Justin Volpe is later convicted and sentenced to thirty years in prison.
- Princess Diana dies in a car crash in Paris.
- A bombing occurs at Otherside Lounge, a lesbian bar in Georgia, by the same White supremacist of the Olympic Park bombing and abortion clinic bombings the prior year.
- The Kyoto Protocol on climate change is adopted.
- Dr. Barnett Slepian, an abortion provider, is assassinated in his home in New York.

1998

- The Lewinsky scandal involving President Bill Clinton becomes public.
- Al Qaeda bombs US embassies in Kenya and Tanzania.
- James Byrd Jr., a Black man, is brutally murdered by White supremacists in Texas.
- Matthew Shephard, a gay college student, is brutally tortured and murdered in Wyoming.
- The US House of Representatives impeaches Bill Clinton.

1999

- Amadou Diallo, an unarmed Guinean immigrant, is shot forty-one times by four NYPD officers as he reaches for his wallet; the officers are acquitted, sparking widespread protests and calls for police reform.
- The Columbine High School shooting occurs in Colorado, killing fifteen and injuring twenty-four people.
- A shooting occurs at North Valley Jewish Community in California by a White supremacist, injuring five people.
- Joseph Ileto, a Filipino American postal worker, is shot and killed by a White supremacist in California, the same White supremacist involved in the North Valley Jewish Community Center shooting.
- Panama regains control of the Panama Canal from the US.
- The world fears the Y2K bug, but major disruptions are avoided.

APPENDIX C

A Few BIPOC Women I Wish I'd
Learned About (Sooner)

Alicia Garza, Patrisse Cullors, and Ayo (formerly Opal) Tometi | These three Black organizers from California and Arizona with intersectional backgrounds are the cofounders of the #BlackLivesMatter movement, set in motion after the acquittal of Trayvon Martin's murderer. Black Lives Matter focuses on fighting racism and anti-Black violence, especially in law enforcement. The movement spread nationally following the murders of Mike Brown and Eric Garner in 2014 at the hands of police. https://blacklivesmatter.com/about/

Audre Lorde (1934–1992) | Born in New York to Caribbean immigrants, Lorde was a writer, professor, intersectional feminist, poet, and civil rights activist. She wrote eighteen books of essays and poetry, including *Sister Outsider,*

one of her most influential books examining racism, sexism, homophobia, and intersectionality.
https://alp.org/about/audre

Brittany Packnett Cunningham (1984–) | Cunningham was born in St. Louis, Missouri, to an ordained minister. She's an activist, organizer, and leader who cofounded Campaign Zero, a policy platform to end police violence. In 2015, *Ebony* named her in its "Power 100" list, and *The Root* featured her in their "Root 100" list.
https://brittanypacknett.com/

Claudette Colvin (1939–2026) | Colvin was born in Alabama during the Jim Crow period. She's a pioneer of the American Civil Rights Movement and a retired nurse aide. She refused to give up her seat on an Alabama bus to a White woman and was arrested for it nine months before Rosa Parks. She was one of the plaintiffs in *Browder v. Gayle*, which ended bus segregation in Alabama.
https://en.wikipedia.org/wiki/Claudette_Colvin

Dr. Dázon Dixon Diallo (1965–) | Born in Fort Valley, Georgia, Diallo was a student in the first integrated classes in her school district. She's now an organizer, a civil rights activist, and advocate of reproductive freedom, as well as a feminist and an AIDS activist. She's also the founder of

SisterLove, the first women's HIV, Sexual and Reproductive Justice organization in the southeastern US, founded in 1989. https://www.sisterlove.org/our-founder

Elizabeth Peratrovich (1911–1958) | Peratrovich was born a member of the Raven Nation in the district of Alaska. She was the Grand President of the Alaska Native Sisterhood, a civil rights activist, and an activist on behalf of Alaskan Natives. Her advocacy led to the passage of Alaska's Anti-Discrimination Act of 1945, the first state antidiscrimination law in the US.
https://en.wikipedia.org/wiki/Elizabeth_Peratrovich

Fannie Lou Hamer (1917–1977) | Born in Mississippi during the Jim Crow period, Hamer became a prominent voice in the civil rights, desegregation, and voting rights movements. She was known for infusing spirituals into protests, such as "This Little Light of Mine" and "Go Tell It on the Mountain," and she was a leader in desegregating the Mississippi Democratic Party.
https://www.womenshistory.org/education-resources/biographies/fannie-lou-hamer

Frances Ellen Watkins Harper (1825–1911) | Harper was born free to free parents. She was a poet, author, lecturer, abolitionist, suffragist, and cofounder of the National

Association of Colored Women's Club. In 1866, she spoke at the National Woman's Rights Convention and delivered her famous speech "We Are All Bound Up Together" in Union Square in New York City.
https://www.womenshistory.org/education-resources/biographies/frances-ellen-watkins-harper

Gloria Anzaldúa (1942–2004) | Born in Texas, Anzaldúa was an educator, activist, and author. She was a Chicana feminist, culture critic, artist, and scholar of queer studies and culture theory. Her best-known book, *Borderlands/La Frontera: The New Mestiza*, is a semiautobiographical work that examines the Chicana/o and Latina/o experiences through the lens of race, gender, identity, and colonialism.
https://gloriaeanzaldua.com/about/

Grace Lee Boggs (1915–2015) | Boggs was born in Rhode Island to immigrant Chinese parents. She was an author, a philosopher, and an activist for civil rights, labor rights, women's rights, environmentalism, and Asian American rights. She epitomized intersectional and inter-movement solidarity and highlighted the shared stakes and power of collective action.
https://en.wikipedia.org/wiki/Grace_Lee_Boggs

Harriet Tubman (1822–1913) | After being born into enslavement and escaping, Tubman became an abolitionist, union spy, military leader, nurse, women's activist, and disability warrior. She was a widely successful conductor with the Underground Railroad who planned and led the military operation at the Combahee River during the Civil War, liberating over 750 enslaved people.

https://www.womenshistory.org/education-resources/biographies/harriet-tubman

Helen Zia (1952–) | Zia was born in New Jersey to Chinese first-generation immigrant parents. She's a journalist, an Asian American activist, and a women's rights activist who cofounded American Citizens for Justice and has published five books on Asian American history, discrimination, and contributions.

https://en.wikipedia.org/wiki/Helen_Zia

Ida B. Wells (1862–1931) | Wells was born into enslavement, and her parents became active in the Reconstruction Era between the end of the Civil War and beginning of Jim Crow laws. She became a prominent researcher, journalist, and activist and was a leader in the anti-lynching movement, a cofounder of the NAACP, and the founder of a Black women's suffrage group.

https://www.womenshistory.org/education-resources/biographies/ida-b-wells-barnett

LaDonna Harris (1931–) | Born a member of the Comanche Nation in Oklahoma, Harris is an activist for Indigenous rights, civil rights, and women's rights. She founded Oklahomans for Indian Opportunity, served on the National Council for Indian Opportunity, and was the first Indigenous woman to run for vice president with the Citizens Party in 1980. https://www.okhistory.org/publications/enc/entry? entry=HA035

Marsha P. Johnson (1945–1992) | Johnson was born in New Jersey to Black parents and assigned a gender that did not align with her identity. She was a drag queen, gay rights activist, and house mother who was known as the "Mayor of Christopher Street." She was a founding member of the Gay Liberation Front, and she cofounded Street Transvestite Action Revolutionaries (STAR) for unhoused gay and trans youth. https://en.wikipedia.org/wiki/Marsha_P._Johnson

Mary Church Terrell (1863–1954) | Born free to formerly enslaved parents, Terrell became a racial justice champion and women's rights activist as an author, a teacher, and a professor. She coined the motto "Lifting as We Climb" for the National Association of Colored Women, which she cofounded and led from 1896 to 1901. In 1940, she published *A Colored Woman in a White World.* https://www.womenshistory.org/education-resources/ biographies/mary-church-terrell

Matilda Joslyn Gage (1826–1898) | Gage was born to abolitionist parents whose home was a station on the Underground Railroad. She was an abolitionist and a suffragette who championed Indigenous rights, and she cofounded the National Woman Suffrage Association with Susan B. Anthony. https://www.womenshistory.org/education-resources/biographies/matilda-joslyn-gage

May Chen (1948–) | Born in Boston, Massachusetts, to immigrant parents from China and Hong Kong, Chen is an educator, a labor organizer, and an advocate for immigration and immigrant workers. She was a union worker, leader, and advocate from the mid-1980s until 2006, and she worked on the International Ladies' Garment Workers' Union Immigrant Project, helping workers gain citizenship. She was also a founding member of the AFL-CIO's Asian Pacific American Labor Alliance. https://en.wikipedia.org/wiki/May_Chen

Nekima Levy Armstong (1976–) | Armstrong was born in Mississippi, grew up in Los Angeles, California, and currently lives in Minneapolis, Minnesota. She's a lawyer, activist, and chairs the Minnesota State Advisory Committee to the US Commission on Civil Rights. She was president of the Minnesota chapter of the NAACP, founded the Community Justice Project, and is a champion of racial justice. https://www.nekimalevyarmstrong.com/

Patsy Mink (1927–2002) | Mink was born in Hawaii and was a third-generation Japanese American. She became an attorney, a champion of both civil rights and women's rights, and a politician. She was the first Woman of Color and the first Asian American woman elected to the US Congress, representing the people of Hawaii from 1965 to 1977 and again from 1990 to 2002. https://www.womenshistory.org/education-resources/biographies/patsy-mink

Rashidah Abdul-Khabeer (formerly Hassan) (1950–) | Abdul-Khabeer was born in Philadelphia to parents who fled Virginia during the Great Migration in the 1920s. She's a nurse, an infectious disease specialist, an activist of both antiracism and AIDS, and an educator. She founded Blacks Educating Blacks About Sexual Health Issues, the first AIDS services organization for and led by Black people. http://afamaidshist.fiu.edu/omeka-s/s/african-american-aids-history-project/item/2549

Rev. Dr. Pauli Murray (1910–1985) | Raised by an extended multiracial family in North Carolina during the Jim Crow period, Murray became a civil rights lawyer, a gender equality lawyer, an author, and an Episcopal priest. Dr. Pauli is legendary in Black liberation, women's, and queer movements. https://www.paulimurraycenter.com/who-is-pauli

Shirley Chisholm (1924–2005) | Chisholm was born in New York to Afro-Guyanese and Afro-Barbadian immigrant parents. She was an organizer, a politician, an activist, and a congresswoman who in 1968 became the first Black woman elected to the US Congress and in 1972 became the first Black woman to run for president of a major party. She was also a founding member of the Congressional Black Caucus and a cofounder of the National Organization of Women.
http://afamaidshist.fiu.edu/omeka-s/s/african-american-aids-history-project/item/2549

Sylvia Rivera (1951–2002) | Born in New York to Puerto Rican and Venezuelan parents, Rivera was assigned a gender that did not align with her identity. She was a drag queen and an activist for gay liberation and transgender rights, and she cofounded Street Transvestite Action Revolutionaries.
https://www.womenshistory.org/education-resources/biographies/sylvia-rivera

Tarana Burke (1973–) | Burke was born in the Bronx, New York, to community organizing parents. She's an activist of civil rights and women's rights, an anti-harassment champion, and an author. She's also the founder of the #MeToo movement against sexual abuse, sexual assault, and rape culture, a demonstration of solidarity among

women who've experienced harm and were pressured to stay silent.
https://metoomvmt.org/get-to-know-us/tarana-burke-founder/

The Combahee River Collective (1974–1980) | A collective of Black feminist lesbians that formed in Boston in response to having their intersectional identity concerns largely ignored and excluded from the feminist and civil rights movements, the members of the Combahee River Collective are credited with developing the concepts of identity politics and laying the foundations for the concept of intersectionality.
https://en.wikipedia.org/wiki/Combahee_River_Collective

Winona LaDuke (1959–) | LaDuke was born in Los Angeles, California, to Sun Bear of the Ojibwe people and Betty Bernstein from the Bronx. She's an environmental, Indigenous, and sustainability activist who helped found the Indigenous Women's Network and founded the White Earth Land Recovery Project.
https://www.womenshistory.org/education-resources/biographies/winona-laduke

Yuri Kochiyama (1921–2014) | Born in California to Japanese parents, Kochiyama became a civil rights and antiwar activist who advocated for reparations for Japanese American internees during WWII after she and her family were interned. She operated in solidarity with other civil rights movements, was close friends with Malcom X, and joined Puerto Rican activists who took over the Statue of Liberty in 1977.

https://www.zinnedproject.org/news/tdih/yuri-kochiyama-was-born/

APPENDIX D

The Five D's of Bystander Intervention

The Five D's of Bystander Intervention

A.K.A. Demonstrating Care to Someone Being Mistreated

Distract

Strike up a conversation with the person being harassed about something innocuous like the weather. Ignore the person who is harassing.

Delegate

Seek support in diffusing by inviting others in the area to interrupt harm. This might be someone with authority in the space space, such as a bus driver, store clerk, or administrator.

Document

Take photos, videos, and/or notes on what is happening. Ask the person being harassed what they would like to do with any materials. Never post or share without their consent.

Delay

Check in on the person after a harassing experience. Let them know you witnessed it and that the behavior was not okay. Ask if they want any support or resources.

Direct

After assessing the physical safety of the situation and environment, stay calm and confront the harasser directly. Keep it short and simple. Redirect your attention to the person who was being harassed.

Originated from <u>Green Dot</u> and <u>Right to Be</u> in 2012

BIBLIOGRAPHY

African American Registry. "The Compromise of 1877, a Story." Accessed June 15, 2024. https://aaregistry.org/story/the-compromise-of-1877-a-short-story/.

Alexander, Michelle. *The New Jim Crow: Mass Incarceration in the Age of Colorblindness.* New Press, 2010.

American Civil Liberties Union (ACLU). "Captive Labor: Exploitation of Incarcerated Workers." June 15, 2022. https://www.aclu.org/publications/captive-labor-exploitation-incarcerated-workers.

Black Panther Party Alumni Legacy Network. "Black Panther Party's Community Survival Programs." Accessed July 14, 2024. https://bppaln.org/programs.

Cassedy, James Gilbert. "African Americans and the American Labor Movement." *Prologue Magazine* 29, no. 2 (Summer 1997). https://www.archives.gov/publications/prologue/1997/summer/american-labor-movement.html.

Center for Advanced Research on Language Acquisition (CARLA). "What Is Culture?" Accessed May 28, 2024. https://archive. carla.umn.edu/culture/definitions.html.

Chandler, David L. "A Good Many Years Before Goodyear." MIT News. May 24, 2010. https://news.mit.edu/2010/ mayaball-0524.

Chinese Railroad Workers in North America Project. "Chinese Railroad Workers in North America Project at Stanford University." Announcement. August 31, 2020. https://web. stanford.edu/group/chineserailroad/cgi-bin/website/.

Coates, Ta-Nehisi. "What We Mean When We Say 'Race Is a Social Construct.'" *The Atlantic.* May 15, 2013. https://www. theatlantic.com/national/archive/2013/05/what-we-mean-when-we-say-race-is-a-social-construct/275872/.

Du Bois, W. E. B. *Black Reconstruction in America: An Essay Toward a History of the Part Which Black Folk Played in the Attempt to Reconstruct Democracy in America, 1860–1880* (Harcourt, Brace and Company, 1935).

Dunbar-Ortiz, Roxanne. *The Indigenous People's History of the United States.* Beacon Press, 2015.

Dunphy, John J. "Charles Lindbergh: Aviator and Extremist." Medium. January 27, 2019. https://johnjdunphy.medium. com/charles-lindbergh-aviator-and-extremist-bdcce12fccbd.

Equal Justice Initiative. "Nixon Adviser Admits War on Drugs Was Designed to Criminalize Black People." March 25, 2016.

https://eji.org/news/nixon-war-on-drugs-designed-to-criminalize-black-people/.

Frail, T. A. "The Injustice of Japanese-American Internment Camps Resonates Strongly to This Day." *Smithsonian Magazine*, January 2017. https://www.smithsonianmag.com/history/injustice-japanese-americans-internment-camps-resonates-strongly-180961422/.

Ghandnoosh, Nazgol. "One in Five: Ending Racial Inequity in Incarceration." The Sentencing Project. October 11, 2023. https://www.sentencingproject.org/reports/one-in-five-ending-racial-inequity-in-incarceration/.

Library of Congress. "African-American Soldiers During the Civil War." *U.S. History Primary Source Timeline: Civil War and Reconstruction, 1861–1877*. Classroom Materials. Accessed June 1, 2024. https://www.loc.gov/classroom-materials/united-states-history-primary-source-timeline/civil-war-and-reconstruction-1861-1877/african-american-soldiers-during-the-civil-war/.

Leone Centre Team. "The Drama Triangle." Psychotherapy Resources. December 27, 2022. https://psychotherapyre-sources.com/discover/relationship-counselling/drama-triangle/.

Logsdon, Jonathan R. "Power, Ignorance, and Anti-Semitism: Henry Ford and His War on Jews." Hanover College History Department. Accessed July 12, 2024. https://history.hanover.edu/hhr/99/hhr99_2.html.

Méndez, Lola. "A Brief Explainer on Latine and Latinx." *Hispanic Executive*, June 5, 2023. https://hispanicexecutive.com/latinx-latine-explainer/.

Morgan, Edmund S. *American Slavery, American Freedom: The Ordeal of Colonial Virginia*. W. W. Norton & Company, 1975.

National Archives. *Executive Order 9066: Resulting in Japanese-American Incarceration (1942)*. Milestone Documents. Accessed July 11, 2024. https://www.archives.gov/milestone-documents/executive-order-9066.

National Women's History Alliance. "Timeline of Legal History of Women in the United States." Accessed July 12, 2024. https://nationalwomenshistoryalliance.org/resources/womens-rights-movement/detailed-timeline/.

NAACP. "The Origins of Modern Day Policing." Accessed June 16, 2024. https://naacp.org/find-resources/history-explained/origins-modern-day-policing.

Okun, Tema. "(divorcing) White Supremacy Culture: Coming Home to Who We Really Are." White Supremacy Culture. Accessed July 30, 2024. https://www.whitesupremacyculture.info/.

Rosenfeld, Alan. "German and Italian Detainees." *Densho Encyclopedia*. Accessed July 11, 2024. https://encyclopedia.densho.org/German_and_Italian_detainees/.

Rothstein, Richard. *The Color of Law: A Forgotten History of How Our Government Segregated America*. Liveright, 2017.

Smithsonian Institution. "Blackface: The Birth of an American Stereotype." National Museum of African American History and Culture. Accessed June 14, 2024. https://nmaahc.si.edu/explore/stories/blackface-birth-american-stereotype.

Smithsonian Institution. "The Historical Legacy of Juneteenth." National Museum of African American History and Culture. Accessed June 16, 2024. https://nmaahc.si.edu/explore/stories/historical-legacy-juneteenth.

United States Department of State. "Repeal of the Chinese Exclusion Act, 1943." Office of the Historian. Milestones: 1937–1945. Accessed July 10, 2024. https://history.state.gov/milestones/1937-1945/chinese-exclusion-act-repeal.

ABOUT THE AUTHOR

Casey Tonnelly (they/them) is a White, nonbinary, queer, disabled, and middle-aged antiracism coach, facilitator, and strategist with nearly two decades of experience working to advance racial and social justice. As the founder of Beyond Thinking, an antiracism coaching and facilitation practice, Casey helps individuals and organizations move beyond intellectual understanding into embodied and sustainable antiracist action.

Before launching Beyond Thinking in 2019, Casey served as a strategic advisor for the City of Seattle for over twelve years, working in the Seattle Office for Emergency Management and the Seattle Office for Civil Rights with the Race and Social Justice Initiative. Their work with the initiative focused on workforce equity, racial equity training, policy consultation, and organizational change efforts.

A certified professional coach, Casey earned their certi-fication through the Institute for Professional Excellence in Coaching in 2019, followed by an Associate Certified Coach accreditation with the International Coaching Federation in 2020 and a Professional Certified Coach accreditation in 2022. Their expertise includes executive coaching, leadership development, antiracism coaching, group coaching, individual and small group coaching, curriculum development, and strategic facilitation.

Casey has worked with a wide range of organizations, including government agencies, nonprofits, and corporate clients, to develop and implement antiracism strategies. They have led initiatives focused on leadership coaching, caucusing, curriculum development, and creating inclusive workplaces.

In addition to their coaching and facilitation work, Casey is the author of *Striving for Anti-Racism: A Beginner's Journal* (2020) and *Still Striving for Anti-Racism: Moving from an Intellectual Understanding to Embodiment* (2023). Their writing and coaching practice reflects a deep commitment to lifelong learning, self-reflection, and the collective work of dismantling systemic oppression.

The B Corp Movement

Dear reader,

Thank you for reading this book and joining the Publish Your Purpose community! You are joining a special group of people who aim to make the world a better place.

What's Publish Your Purpose About?
Our mission is to elevate the voices often excluded from traditional publishing. We intentionally seek out authors and storytellers with diverse backgrounds, life experiences, and unique perspectives to publish books that will make an impact in the world.

Beyond our books, we are focused on tangible, action-based change. As a woman- and LGBTQ+-owned company, we are committed to reducing inequality, lowering levels of poverty, creating a healthier environment, building stronger communities, and creating high-quality jobs with dignity and purpose.

As a Certified B Corporation, we use business as a force for good. We join a community of mission-driven companies building a more equitable, inclusive, and sustainable global economy. B Corporations must meet high standards of transparency, social and environmental performance, and accountability as determined by the nonprofit B Lab. The certification process is rigorous and ongoing (with a recertification requirement every three years).

How Do We Do This?
We intentionally partner with socially and economically disadvantaged businesses that meet our sustainability goals. We embrace and encourage our authors and employee's differences in race, age, color, disability, ethnicity, family or marital status, gender identity or expression, language, national origin, physical and mental ability, political affiliation, religion, sexual orientation, socio-economic status, veteran status, and other characteristics that make them unique.

Community is at the heart of everything we do—from our writing and publishing programs to contributing to social enterprise nonprofits like reSET (https://www.resetco.org/) and our work in founding B Local Connecticut.

We are endlessly grateful to our authors, readers, and local community for being the driving force behind the equitable and sustainable world we are building together.

To connect with us online, or publish with us,
visit us at www.publishyourpurpose.com.

Elevating Your Voice,

Jenn T. Grace
Founder, Publish Your Purpose